STRUGGLING FOR ETHNIC IDENTITY

The Gypsies of Hungary

Helsinki Watch

Human Rights Watch
New York • Washington • Los Angeles • London

Library of Congress Card Catalogue No.: 93-079631
ISBN: 1-56432-112-6

Cover photograph: copyright © Csaba Toroczkay. Roma men at a July 13, 1993 demonstration, the largest of the post-war era, held in Eger, Hungary to protest skinhead attacks against Romas.

HUMAN RIGHTS WATCH

Human Rights Watch conducts regular, systematic investigations of human rights abuses in some sixty countries around the world. It addresses the human rights practices of governments of all political stripes, of all geopolitical alignments, and of all ethnic and religious persuasions. In internal wars it documents violations by both governments and rebel groups. Human Rights Watch defends freedom of thought and expression, due process of law and equal protection of the law; it documents and denounces murders, disappearances, torture, arbitrary imprisonment, exile, censorship and other abuses of internationally recognized human rights.

Human Rights Watch began in 1978 with the founding of Helsinki Watch by a group of publishers, lawyers and other activists and now maintains offices in New York, Washington, D.C., Los Angeles, London, Moscow, Belgrade, Zagreb and Hong Kong. Today, it includes Africa Watch, Americas Watch, Asia Watch, Helsinki Watch, Middle East Watch, the Fund for Free Expression and three collaborative projects, the Arms Project, Prison Project and Women's Rights Project. Human Rights Watch is an independent, nongovernmental organization, supported by contributions from private individuals and foundations. It accepts no government funds, directly or indirectly.

The executive committee includes Robert L. Bernstein, chair; Adrian W. DeWind, vice chair; Roland Algrant, Lisa Anderson, Peter D. Bell, Alice Brown, William Carmichael, Dorothy Cullman, Irene Diamond, Jonathan Fanton, Jack Greenberg, Alice H. Henkin, Stephen L. Kass, Marina Pinto Kaufman, Alexander MacGregor, Bruce Rabb, Orville Schell, Gary Sick, Malcolm Smith and Robert Wedgeworth.

The staff includes Kenneth Roth, acting executive director; Holly J. Burkhalter, Washington director; Gara LaMarche, associate director; Susan Osnos, press director; Ellen Lutz, California director; Jemera Rone, counsel; Stephanie Steele, operations director; Michal Longfelder, development director; Allyson Collins, research associate; Joanna Weschler, Prison Project director; Kenneth Anderson, Arms Project director; and Dorothy Q. Thomas, Women's Rights Project director.

The executive directors of the divisions of Human Rights Watch are Abdullahi An-Na'im, Africa Watch; Juan E. Méndez, Americas Watch; Sidney Jones, Asia Watch; Jeri Laber, Helsinki Watch; Andrew Whitley, Middle East Watch; and Gara LaMarche, the Fund for Free Expression.

Addresses for Human Rights Watch
485 Fifth Avenue
New York, NY 10017-6104
Tel: (212) 972-8400
Fax: (212) 972-0905
email: hrwatchnyu@igc.org

10951 West Pico Blvd., #203
Los Angeles, CA 90064
Tel: (310) 475-3070
Fax: (310) 475-5613
email: hrwatchla@igc.org

1522 K Street, N.W., #910
Washington, DC 20005
Tel: (202) 371-6592
Fax: (202) 371-0124
email: hrwatchdc@igc.org

90 Borough High Street
London, UK SE1 1LL
Tel: (071) 378-8008
Fax: (071) 378-8029
email: africawatch@gn.org

CONTENTS

ACKNOWLEDGEMENTS

This report is based on a mission conducted by Gyorgy Feher, a consultant for Helsinki Watch, in January of 1993. The report was written by Mr. Feher and edited by Holly Cartner and Lois Whitman.

Helsinki Watch expresses its appreciation to all those who contributed to this report. Particular thanks are due to Jozsef Gobolyos for his contribution to the research of the report, and to Gabor Noszkai for his invaluable assistance. In addition, Helsinki Watch would like to thank the Human Rights Internship Program of Columbia University and its director, Deborah Greenberg.

PREFACE

Since the demise of the Communist regime in Hungary, the country's Roma population has benefitted from the suspension of decades of assimilationist, and at times overtly racist, government policy and from an increased tolerance for expression of Roma identity. The amended Hungarian Constitution recognizes Gypsies' equality under the law and acknowledges the need for affirmative action measures to counteract the effects of their history of repression; and a Law on the Rights of National and Ethnic Minorities was passed on July 7, 1993, after nearly two years of parliamentary debate. However, Romas continue to suffer serious discrimination, and at times violence, at the hands of fellow citizens, and many public officials appear to exhibit the same behavior.

In Hungary today, Roma living standards are substantially lower than those of the ethnic Hungarian population, primarily because their access to jobs, as well as to housing and education, is to some extent dictated by their ethnicity. A disproportionate number of them are among the country's growing contingent of unemployed workers, and many allege that they are the victims of discriminatory labor practices. In regions in which Romas are the minority, local housing councils systematically discriminate against them, excluding them from placement rosters or allocating to them the worst of the available housing. Conditions in predominately Roma villages can be even worse, as many of them lack basic amenities, such as schools, health facilities and municipal services, that are available in most other areas. Also, many Romas face discrimination in their daily social dealings, ranging from restricted access to bars and nightclubs to exclusion from community organizations.

Finally, and most seriously, Romas are more vulnerable than other ethnic groups to violence both by public officials and private citizens. They are increasingly singled out as targets for violence by skinheads and other militant nationalists, and public authorities have not responded adequately, either in apprehending or prosecuting the offenders. Moreover, the use of excessive force and unlawful detention at the hands of the police appear to be more prevalent against Romas than against ethnic Hungarians, as the authorities apparently act out the widely-held racist stereotype of Romas as dishonest and violent. Romas' lack of representation and effective political voice, coupled with a mistrust of the impartiality of public authority, has limited their ability to seek redress in these cases.

INTRODUCTION

Europe's Roma peoples have long been a forgotten and misunderstood minority - indeed the commonly used English designation "Gypsy," its Hungarian, French, Spanish, German etc. equivalents ("Cigany," "Tsigane," "Zigeuner," "Gitano" etc.) arose out of an erroneous identification of these nomadic people migrating from northern India sometime during the 11th century A.D. and arriving to Europe by the 14th century. Most scholars suggest that the etymology derives from "Egypt," given that non-Christian invaders of the European continent during the middle ages, with whom the Romas may have been confused, were occasionally labelled "Egyptian," a generic name given to "heathens," Muslims and exotic peoples of the East. Others maintain that the name is derived from Gyppe, a site of a large Roma settlement near Methoni, Greece or that the word derives from the Greek "atsingkanoi" or "athinganoi," meaning "untouchable."[1]

Since the word "Gypsy" is increasingly held to be pejorative,[2] this report will use the term "Roma" whenever possible. It should be noted though that the majority of Hungary's Romas still find the designation "Gypsy" acceptable and that among the one hundred plus Roma organized associations more than half employ the term "Gypsy."[3]

---

[1] Compare Ian Hancock, "The East-European Roots of Romani Nationalism," in Henry R. Huttenbach (ed.) The Gypsies in Eastern Europe, *Nationalities Paper* (Special Issue), Fall 1991 at 253, and Ian Hancock, "The Romani Diaspora: Part I," *The World and I*, March 1989 at 614 with Gyorgy Rostas-Farkas, Ciganysagomat vallalom ("Grizhij muro romanipe") Kossuth Konyvkiado, Budapest 1992 at 16 and Francois de Vaux de Foletier, "A Ciganyok Vilaga" ("The World of the Gypsies") excerpted from Le Monde de Tsigane, in *Phralipe* No. 9, 1991 at 7-11. On "atsingkanoi" see Miklos Tomka, "A ciganyok tortenete" ("The History of Gypsies") in Laszlo Szego (ed.) *Ciganyok: honnet jottek, merre tartanak (Gypsies: where do they come from where are they heading)* at 37, Kozmosz Konyvek, Budapest 1983.

[2] The use of the term "Gypsy" was condemned at the first World Romani Congress, April 8-12, 1971, London, England.

[3] "Hungarian Gypsy Associations" compiled in December 1992 by the Office of National and Ethnic Minorities.

1

While Hungary's Romas possess a common historical and linguistic origin, they do not comprise a homogenous group. In the past, Romas classified one another according to dialects, professions and membership in social organizations, an elaborate taxonomy reflecting their cultural heterogeneity. Successive waves of forced assimilation eradicated much of this diversity, however, and today language-use is probably the most apparent division among Hungary's Romas. About three-quarters are monolingual Hungarian speakers (in Romany the so-called "Romungros"), with the Romany speaking Olach (or Olah) comprising around one-fifth, while the rest speak a 19th century version of Romanian (the Beash), though Olah and Beash speakers are generally fluent in Hungarian as well.[4]

The Roma population of Hungary has been frequently estimated but its exact size remains a point of some contention. Censuses of the past used language or nationality as the criteria for counting Romas which skewed the results by classifying Romungros (and possibly the Beash) as non-Roma. The 1980 Census, for instance, registered some 27,000 who spoke Romany as their native tongue, while only some 6,400 identified themselves as members of a "Gypsy nationality." Accordingly, recent studies define Gypsy as "one who is regarded as such by the non-Gypsy surroundings on the basis of various criteria (such as life-style, physical appearance)." This definition yielded an estimate of some 320,000 Romas in 1971. The 1990 Census, using a similar definition, estimated the Roma population to be around 400,000. Most other scholarly studies produce estimates of between 420,000-500,000, with 450,000 the recurring estimate, which appears to be the most reliable figure.[5]

---

[4] On common historical and linguistic origin see e.g., Ian Hancock, "The Romani Diaspora," *op. cit.*; David Crowe, "The Roma (Gypsies) in Hungary Through the Kadar Era," in Henry R. Huttenbach (ed.) *op. cit.*, 297-312. The extent of non-Hungarian speaking minority remains disputed. Compare Anna Csongor, "Cigany gyerekek az iskolaban," ("Gypsy children in the schools") (manuscript) at 1 (small number of Roma children don't speak Hungarian) with Crowe *op. cit.* at 303 (vast numbers don't speak Hungarian).

[5] On 1980 Census figure *see* Karoly Kocsis and Zoltan Kovacs, "A magyarorszagi ciganynepesseg tarsadolomfoldrajza" ("The social geography of Hungary's gypsy population") in Agnes Utasi and Agnes Meszaros (eds.) *Ciganylet* (*Gypsy life*) MTA, Budapest, 1991 at 79; the "Gypsy" definition and 1971 estimate

Prior to the jump-start industrialization of Hungary in the 1950s, the overwhelming majority of the Romas were rural. By the 1980s the proportion of urbanized Romas grew to around forty percent with significant regional variations. In Szabolcs-Szatmar-Bereg county in the northeast, bordering the Ukraine, six out of seven Romas are still living in the country, while in Vas county three out of four Romas are urbanized. The largest Roma urban centers are Budapest, with at least 50,000 Roma residents, Miskolc (17,000) and Ozd (10,000, the highest percentage of Romas in an urban center). There are nearly 700 settlements where Romas constitute around one tenth of the population. Romas comprise a quarter of the population in one hundred villages or so and in a dozen or so, mostly in the northeast, Romas are the majority.[6]

This report begins with a brief overview of the history of Hungary's Romas from their arrival in what is now Hungary to the present day. Subsequent sections will examine past and present conditions of the Romas in areas such as education, housing, employment, health care, relations with the police, portrayal in the media and in popular culture. Roma political and cultural rights and their ability to enforce those rights, during the communist regime and subsequent to the emergence of a democratic republic in 1990 will also be examined. Special emphasis will be placed on disturbing new trends, notably the significant increase in anti-Roma sentiments, intensification of communal strife between Romas and non-Romas and the growth of overtly racist attacks directed at Romas.

---

is that of Istvan Kemenyi, *Beszamolo a magyarorszagi ciganyok helyzetevel foglalkozo 1971-ben vegzett kutatasrol* (*Report of the 1971 Research dealing with the situation of Hungarian gypsies*) MTA, Budapest, 1976 at 291. For 1990 estimate see *Facts Sheets on Hungary* No. 9, at 2, Ministry of Foreign Affairs, Budapest, 1991.

[6] *See* Kocsis and Kovacs *op. cit.* at 90.

STRUGGLE FOR ETHNIC IDENTITY:
A HISTORICAL OVERVIEW

The first major wave of Romas appeared in Hungary during the reign of King Zsigmond (Sigismund 1387-1437), the majority of whom continued to migrate to western Europe. Over the course of the next century and a half, as they were systematically expelled from the western lands, Romas began to settle in the Carpathian basin. During the Ottoman occupation of Hungary, spanning some 150 years till the late 17th century, Romas had a measure of autonomy and began to specialize in certain sedentary trades, working as blacksmiths, weapon-makers, horse traders, carpenters and barbers. Little is known of Roma culture of the period or of Roma relations with the non-Romas (the "gadzikane" in Romany or "gaje"[7]), though it appears that segregation into ghettoes was widespread.

Subsequent to the defeat of the Ottoman Turks, the Habsburg monarchy initiated an aggressive assimilationist campaign. This was based on a mixture of rewards, such as residency and trade permits, and punishments, notably the prohibition of the itinerant lifestyle (1761 edict of Maria-Theresa), a ban of the use of Roma names (1761) and the Romany language (by Joseph II in 1783) and forced adoptions of Roma children by non-Roma families.

As a result of assimilation coupled with an upsurge in migration of Romas seeking to escape these policies, the Roma population fell and did not recover until the mid-19th century, when Hungary received an influx of Romanian Roma.[8]

Post-Trianon[9] Hungary initiated a fierce "magyarization" policy, pressuring "sedentary" Romas to become fully assimilated and taking

---

[7] Gaje (plural), gajo (sing., mas.) and gaji (sing. fem.).

[8] *See* Miklos Tomka *op. cit.*, 36-52; B. Mezey et. al (eds.), *A magyarorszagi ciganykerdes dokumentumokban 1422-1985 (The Hungarian gypsy question in documents 1422-1985)*, at 12-19, 75-76, Kossuth Konyvkiado, Budapest 1986; Jozsef Vekerdi, "Earliest Arrival Evidence on Gypsies in Hungary," 170-171, *Journal of the Gypsy Lore Society*, Vol. I, No. 2 (1971).

[9] The 1918 Treaty which dismantled the Austro-Hungarian empire and created Hungary's present day borders.

draconian police measures to deport Romas whose Hungarian citizenship could not be verified. As a decree of the Ministry of Interior stated: "Special attention must be paid by the police and security organs to ensure that the wandering Gypsies, or other wandering groups, should not even be allowed near the cities."[10]

Little is known about the fate of Hungary's Romas during the Holocaust (or "Porajmos") most of whom, akin to Hungary's Jewish population, were deported to various concentration camps and exterminated after Germany's 1944 invasion of Hungary. The number of European and Hungarian Romas murdered remains unknown; some maintain that around a quarter of Europe's one million Romas were exterminated while others estimate the figure to have been closer to 500,000. Estimates on the number of Hungarian Romas murdered vary from 60,000-70,000 to 20,000-30,000, though a recent study suggests that the number may have been lower, around 5,000.[11]

Romas were excluded from the post World-War II land redistributions and were persecuted, along with other minorities, for their attempt to assert an ethnic identity. In 1961, however, the Communist Party[12] suddenly acknowledged the existence of a "Gypsy problem." Refuting the 1960 Census which found only 25,000 "Gypsies," the party now acknowledged in a resolution that the Romas numbered more than 200,000, though the "Gypsies" were not recognized as a national or ethnic minority. Instead they were identified as a "disadvantaged social stratum," classified into "assimilated," "quasi-assimilated" and "non-assimilated"

---

[10] BM Korrendelet 257.000/1928, reprinted in Mezey *et. al.* (eds.), *op cit.*, at 200-201.

[11] The 500,000 estimate is by Henry R. Huttenbach, "The Romani Porajmos: The Nazi Genocide of Europe's Gypsies," at 373-391 in Henry. R. Huttenbach (ed.) *op cit*; The 60,000-70,000 figure is supplied by the Roma Parliament (Helsinki Watch interview, January 6, 1993); 20,000-30,000 is by David Crowe *op. cit.* at 298 and Janos Szonyi, "A ciganyok sorsa a fasizmus evei alatt," ("The fate of the Gypsies during the fascist years,") at 53-57 in Laszlo Szego *op. cit.* The 5,000 figure is by Laszlo Karsai, *A Ciganykerdes Magyarorszagon 1919-1945 (Ut a cigany Holocausthoz), (The Gypsy question in Hungary (The road to the Gypsy Holocaust))* at 12-13, 85-112, *Scientia Hungariae*, Cserepfalvi, Budapest, 1992.

[12] the Hungarian Socialist Workers' Party or MSZMP by its Hungarian acronym.

groups, and the party announced its goal to "take up the gauntlet against the prevailing prejudices which impede the Gypsies' assimilation."[13]

The main pillars of the assimilation program were employment, housing and education. Integration into the labor force, in which fewer than one in four Roma men participated fully, became a rallying call. Throughout the 1960s thousands of Romas were recruited, primarily into the mining, heavy industries and agricultural sector, usually performing the most demanding, dangerous and least paid tasks. The transformation was dramatic. By 1971 nine out of ten Roma men, and four out of ten Roma women, on average, were fully employed. But the costs borne by the Romas were immense. The proportion of Romas on invalid pension exceeded two to three times the national average, while life-expectancy of Romas remains today some twelve years lower than for other Hungarians. Industrial employment has also created social dislocation as the shortage of housing in the industrial centers forced many Roma men to move to workers' shelters for years, far removed from their families. Moreover, those Romas who sought to advance beyond the least prestigious industrial occupations confronted considerable obstacles; in the army, for instance, Romas were almost invariably assigned to the labor battalions, foreclosing all opportunities for professional advancement.[14]

The 1961 resolution also recognized that the housing conditions of Hungary's Romas required immediate attention. Nearly two-thirds of all Romas lived in dilapidated houses in ghettoized shanty-towns, with several generations sharing a room, usually with no indoor toilets,

---

[13] MSZMP resolutions are reprinted in Mezey et. al. (eds.) *op. cit.*, 240-318; 1961 resolution is at 240-242.

[14] Employment trends: MSZMP resolutions reprinted in Mezey et. al. (eds.) *loc. cit*; David Crowe *op. cit.*, 302; Agnes Diosi, "Legyen Vilagossag," ("Let There Be Light"), *Kritika*, January 1993 at 4; life expectancy estimate is from Katalin Pik, "A Halal Nem Valogat," ("Death does not Choose") *Phralipe* No. 7 1991 and "A munkavegzes es az egeszsegi allapot osszefugese," ("The connection between employment and health conditions") in Utasi and Meszaros (eds.) *op. cit.* at 163. Pension estimates are from Helsinki Watch interview with Ivan Szelenyi, sociologist, July 20, 1992. On army discrimination: Helsinki Watch interviews with Aladar Horvath, President of Roma Parliament, January 6, 1993, Ottilia Solt, Member of Parliament (SZDSZ), January 5, 1993, Janos Ladanyi, January 4, 1993, sociologist.

frequently without any running or at least potable water and with one-third of dwellings lacking electricity. In response, the government launched an ambitious slum and ghetto eradication program in 1964, as a result of which the number of slum dwellings fell from over 50,000 to around 5,000 by 1984, with a corresponding drop in occupants from around 250,000 (of whom well over three-quarters were Romas) to around 40,000. Slum-clearance was supplemented by the supply of credit for new constructions of approximately 20,000 family dwellings, which the government envisioned as facilitating Roma assimilation into their non-Roma surroundings.

These statistics, however, overstate the actual achievements of the program. While the isolated Roma rural ghettos ("ciganytelep") were largely eradicated, they were often reconstituted elsewhere as Roma influx into neighborhoods led to a corresponding outflow of local non-Romas. Moreover, public housing funds were funneled in a manner which did not always aid the intended Roma beneficiaries. Some local councils spent the money on purchasing existing dwellings from non-Roma residents and re-selling them to Romas at subsidized interest. Though Romas received decent housing in these instances, the prices paid by councils were often so inflated that most of the subsidies ended up lining the pocket of the non-Roma sellers. Elsewhere, paternalistic councils transferred the money to contractors (Romas were seen as too irresponsible to handle their finances), who engaged in a variety of practices aimed at pocketing the public funds.

As the assimilationist ideology waned in the 1980s, deliberate ghettoization occasionally resurfaced as a response to the "Gypsy problem." In 1988, for instance, officials in Miskolc, a large industrial town in north-east Hungary, attempted to transfer the large Roma community living in the inner city to a high-rise project constructed at a remote site. Public outcry eventually led to the abandonment of the project.[15]

---

[15] On ghetto eradication and re-creation se David Crowe *op. cit.*, 301; Katalin Berey, "A ciganytelepek felszamolasa es ujratermelodese," ("Eradication and regeneration of gypsy slums") in Utasi and Meszaros (eds.) *op. cit.* 106-143; Anna Csongor in Adras Toth and Gabor Laszlo (eds.) Beyond the Great Transformation, *Review of Hungarian Social Sciences* 1991/2 at 206; on misuse of public funds, Helsinki Watch interview with Bea Morvai, January 14, 1993, case worker with SZETA. On the Miskolc ghetto *see* Janos Ladanyi, "Ethnic

Improvement of the educational level of Romas was another priority for the Socialist Workers' Party. Over 40 percent of Romas were estimated to be functionally illiterate and the drop-out rate among Roma children was extraordinarily high; on average, only one in ten Roma children advanced into high school in contrast with the non-Roma population, among which nine out of ten enrolled in high school. The state responded by establishing special "Gypsy classes," institutionalizing Roma children in "special-education" facilities and by imposing severe penalties on parents who failed to ensure regular school attendance by their children.

The motives and methods of the government policy remain hotly contested to the present; while Roma retention rates have improved dramatically and functional illiteracy has dropped markedly, the intra-school segregation of Roma children has not abated. Nor did this segregation produce expected benefits of "positive discrimination" because Roma classes and schools were usually overcrowded, often led by uncaring or poorly qualified teachers, many of whom were assigned to "Gypsy classes" as a form of punishment. [16]

Although the Janos Kadar era's assimilationist policy[17] did not tolerate Roma attempts to develop an ethnic or nationalist identity[18] it did permit cultural expressions which it perceived as either innocuous or,

---

discrimination and self-protection: the case of the Gipsies living in the city of Miskolc," *Valosag*, 1991/3 and *Revue Scientifique Internationale*, vol. 69 at 113-128 (1991).

[16] On Roma retention rates: William O. McCagg *op. cit.*, 323; David Crowe, *op. cit.* 303; Anna Csongor, "Cigany osztalyok Magyarorszagon," ("Gypsy classes in Hungary") *Phralipe* No. 10 1991; Anna Csongor, "A cigany gyerekek iskolai," ("The schools of Gypsy children") in Meszaros and Utasi (eds.) *op. cit.*, 179-200; Anna Csongor and Peter Szuhay, *loc. cit.*; Helsinki Watch interview with Anna Csongor January 4, 1993; Istvan Kotnyek, "A cigany gyermekek oktatasa Magyarorszagon," ("The education of the Gypsy children in Hungary") in Szego (ed.), *op. cit.*, 305; On "Gypsy classes" as a form of punishment *see* Anna Csongor, "Cigany gyerekek az iskolaban," *op. cit.*, at 6.

[17] Janos Kadar headed the MSZMP from 1956 until 1988.

[18] *See, e.g.*, MSZMP KB resolution of April 18, 1979 reprinted in Mezey. et. al., (eds.), *op. cit.*, at 265-269.

perhaps, as too difficult to suppress. Thus, Romas were allowed to perform their songs and dances and several associations were set up by the state to finance and control Roma activities.

Between 1961 and the mid 1980s, the Socialist Workers' Party also sought to combat anti-Roma prejudice, an undertaking destined for failure given that the party's conception of the "Gypsy problem" itself was rooted in an ideology which espoused many of those prejudices. As one expert stated, for instance:

> Although we dismiss the concept of biological determinism, we state on the basis of the proofs of modern genetics that a human being's individual characteristics are partially determined by genotypes. Hence in the case of Gypsies the historical factors (the ethical outlook brought from India, their wandering and despised status etc.) do not exclude the possibility that certain negative characteristics (stealing, begging etc.) are inherited from parents to children.[19]

Or, as another author reviewing the Party's measures in a positive light suggested:

> There are several factors that preclude the necessary cooperation between Gypsy and other school children in integrated schools. Perhaps one of the most important is that Gypsy children do not like to engage in communal play . . . [a]nother fundamental gap existing between Gypsy and other children is that Gypsies at school age find it difficult to understand any kind of abstraction. Abstract terms, even the concept of time, seem to be outside of the grasp of Gypsies.[20]

Less egregiously offensive analyses of the Roma condition still condemned the Romas' insistence to maintain their ethnic and cultural

---

[19] Elemer Varnagy, quoted by Csongor and Szuhay, *op. cit.*, at 238.

[20] Francis S. Wagner, "The Gypsy Problem in Postwar Hungary," *Hungarian Studies Review*, Vol. XIV, No. 2 (Fall 1987) at 40.

identity as "misguided attempts." However, the official sociology was increasingly challenged by a dissident intellectual movement during the 1970s and especially the 1980s:

> The Kadarist authorities sought to stifle pro-Gypsy criticism of what they were doing. But by then the cat was out of the bag. They had permitted the reemergence of sociology in the country and had encouraged sociological investigations of the Gypsy problem. As a result, it was widely recognized in intelligentsia circles not only that the Gypsies were poor, but also that poverty existed in this Socialist country . . . By the middle 1970s, one of the first of Hungary's opposition groups, the SZETA,[21] had crystallized around the sociologists' Gypsy project; and in the early 1980s the Sociological Institute's much broader investigation of the poverty problem in Hungary spearheaded the ideological bankruptcy of the regime.[22]

---

[21] Established in 1977 and operating illegally until 1988, SZETA, or Szegenyeket Tamogato Alap (Foundation to Support the Poor), aids families in need, most of which are Romas.

[22] William D. McCagg, *op. cit.*, 328.

BEYOND COMMUNISM:
THE STRUGGLE OF THE ROMAS TODAY

The socio-economic status of Romas since the fall of communism

Since the fall of the communist regime the economic situation of Hungary's Romas has worsened dramatically. While the economic restructuring of a command economy into a western style market economy created hardships for most Hungarians, with the national unemployment rate heading toward 14 percent[23] and per capita real income falling, the burdens imposed on Romas are disproportionately great. The unemployment rate among Hungary's Romas is now between 60 and 70 percent of adult males and in some regions, especially in the rural areas of the northeast, the rate is between 80 and 100 percent.[24]

But even among villages with high unemployment rates the differences in living conditions may be enormous. Where Romas comprise a minority, their settlements at least have access to schools, health-care and municipal services. In contrast, there are dozens of villages which are now overwhelmingly populated by Romas where the exodus of non-Roma peasants was followed by the withdrawal of basic amenities. Some of the Romas left behind may qualify for unemployment insurance, which provides a modicum of income for a limited period. Others are forced to fend off starvation by foraging for food, scavenging for scrap metal or by migrating to other villages or towns. At the most extreme, as in the village of Bogacs, several of the 300 Roma inhabitants have resorted to self-mutilation. As one middle-aged man explained to a television crew:

> I cut my finger off, I had to, I was hungry . . . [t]hat's how it is, do you hear? No one supports us except God almighty! I put it [the finger] down on the concrete here,

---

[23] February 18, 1993 BBC Summary of World Broadcasts; Part 2 Eastern Europe; Weekly Economic Report; HUNGARY PAGE: EE/W0269/A ;SOURCE: Hungarian Radio, Budapest home service 1200 gmt, February 12, 1993.

[24] *HVG*, January 2, 1993 at 55-57; *Amaro Drom*, 1992/11 at 9; "Gypsies in the Labor Market," (manuscript) available from Roma Parliament, Budapest.

and with one swing of the axe, it's gone, then a little blood comes out, not much. Then I go to the doctor, he sews it up, or doesn't give a fuck, who cares, it'll heal, it's going to rot away one day anyway, even like this . . . man just rots anyway . . . we do it out of necessity, hunger, the hunger brings it on. I'd cut the other four off too if I wouldn't get fined for it, if they'd pay me something.[25]

Although such drastic measures are admittedly very rare, as are instances of starvation,[26] abject poverty is a growing phenomenon among the Romas in rural areas.

Changes in the education system have been more promising. The teaching of Romany is now permitted though its scale remains limited due to financial constraints. In addition, a private foundation is planning to open Hungary's first private all-Roma high school in September 1993 in the city of Pecs.[27] Moreover, the city's university is also expected to introduce a "ciganologia" (i.e. Roma studies) course in the near future.[28]

Concurrently, the government has allocated 16,500 HUF (approximately $200) per Roma student in the 1993 education budget, in addition to the per capita subsidy provided to all school children.[29] Still, some Roma advocates perceive this aid as both inadequate and inappropriate. As Anna Csongor, an education specialist who has written extensively about the problems faced by Romas, commented to Helsinki Watch:

---

[25] PILOT Productions 1992. Transcripts available.

[26] There are some villages, such as Monor as well as Csenyete, an overwhelmingly Roma hamlet near Miskolc where charity organizations supply at least some of the food, or the money for its purchase, for most of the locals. *New Hungarian Quarterly, loc. cit.*; Ivan Szelenyi, "Making of the rural underclass: the Gypsy village ghetto-poor of Csenyete," (manuscript) 1992.

[27] *Magyar Hirlap*, April 23, 1992.

[28] *Amaro Drom*, 1993/1.

[29] Republic of Hungary, 1993 Budget Volume I.

First, I'm not convinced that per capita aid is the appropriate way to go about helping Gypsies when there are many schools - especially in the countryside - which are so run down, lacking so many essential facilities, and I mean desks and chairs, that the money ought to be allocated differently. Second, the money is given not specifically for the purpose of, say, language teaching but to bring about the 'catching up of Gypsies, individually or as a group,' a formulation which stigmatizes by suggesting that Gypsies are somehow backward by nature . . . It would have been preferable to give aid to Gypsies with no strings attached or to give it to only those with, say, reading difficulties - in which case, of course, it would still go largely to Gypsy children . . . Finally, the government is now for the first time introducing fees for higher education - especially technical education and such fees, in the absence of some privately-funded scholarship, would prevent many Gypsy youths from even trying their luck with technical training.

However, most commentators suggest that the greatest present obstacle is not even the quality of education received by Romas, but their inability to get jobs irrespective of their qualification. In an adverse economic climate, in the absence of affirmative action policies, most young Romas have no prospects whatsoever. As one distraught mother in the town of Debrecen complained to Helsinki Watch:

I taught my daughter that as a Gypsy she would have to work harder to get results. She wanted to go to technical school or become a nurse but they would not take her. Her school-mistress said as a Gypsy she shouldn't even think of going to the "gimnazium" [an advanced secondary school] because she couldn't cope and would only be crushed . . . well, I yelled and screamed till she got her recommendation . . . and she went to the gimnazium . . . and she worked hard and got good grades . . . and now? Now nothing. She is sitting at home, crying her eyes out because there is no work, though she's been looking for six months now.

out because there is no work, though she's been looking for six months now.

In contrast to educational changes, the housing situation of Romas has clearly worsened. Though the pace of housing construction was always slow, since the fall of communism new construction has essentially ceased. Even more devastating has been the gradual whittling away of local government subsidies of rents, electricity and fuel which adversely affected all poor people, a large percentage of whom are Roma. Moreover, as state industries close down or are privatized they sell off their "worker-hostels," which provided temporary homes for thousands of Roma men, many of whom have now become homeless. As a result, Roma families increasingly seek out abandoned buildings, a temporary solution at best, especially as local councils quickly evict such squatters.[30] Given that urban migration, especially to Budapest, is intensifying, the prospects of Romas for securing adequate housing appear very bleak.[31]

The legal situation of Romas

Hungary's political transformation began with the so-called Opposition Roundtable discussions of June 1989 between the communists and a coalition of dissident movements. It then proceeded with the constitutional amendment of October 1989,[32] and culminated with the holding of free parliamentary elections in March 1990. The ethnic and national minority issues received detailed attention. Act XVII was passed

---

[30] See, e.g., *Nepszabadsag*, December 21, 1991, reporting the eviction of forty families in the city of Miskolc. Also see discussion below.

[31] See, e.g., Gabor Csanadi and Janos Ladanyi, *Budapest terbeni-tarsadalmi szerkezetenek valtozasai* (*Changes in Budapest's spatial-societal structure*) Akademia Konyvkiado Budapest 1992.

[32] The Act of Constitutional Amendment No XXXI (1989) was voted and approved by the communist dominated Parliament prior to the legalization of opposition parties. The Constitution has been amended on a number of occasions since October 1989 and now approximately 90 percent of it has been revised.

two as members of the opposition Free Democrats, while a third sits with the Socialists.[33]

The amended Constitution confers a broad array of rights and protections on all Hungarian citizens. Article 68 recognizes the equality of all national and ethnic minorities, guarantees their collective participation in public affairs, and safeguards the nurturing of their national or ethnic cultures and the use and teaching of their native languages. The Constitution also recognizes the need for affirmative discrimination by authorizing the election of national and ethnic minority representatives to Parliament[34] and granting ethnic and national minority autonomy in the form of "minority self-governments."

On June 3, 1992 the Constitutional Court held Parliament to be in contempt of its constitutional obligations for failing to enact a law on minorities and urged Parliament to pass legislation by December 1, 1992. An Office of National and Ethnic Minorities was established in the fall of 1990 by the coalition government[35] to consult with the Minorities Roundtable - representing Hungary's national and ethnic minorities - in drafting such a bill. However, the consensus initially forged quickly began to dissipate. The August 1991 draft ("Consensus Draft"), which had the stamp of the Roundtable's approval, was significantly modified in February 1992, provoking so much opposition that it was finally withdrawn in April 1992. Another draft, prepared in June 1992, was submitted to Parliament in its place.

The controversy surrounding the Minority Bill revolved around three main issues: the definition of national and ethnic minorities, the blueprint offered for minority autonomy in the form of "self-governments" and parliamentary representation, and the nature of financial guarantees.

---

[33] Aladar Horvath (SZDSZ), President of the Roma Parliament, Antonia Haga (SZDSZ) and Tamas Peli (MSZP).

[34] Article 68. § (3) and Article 70/A. § (2).

[35] Comprising the Hungarian Democratic Forum (MDF), Independent Smallholders (FKgP) and Christian Democrats (KDNP).

Chapter I of the consensus draft (August 1991)[36] identified minorities, for the purpose of protection under the act, as any group indigenous to Hungary which constitutes a numerical minority within the local population, whose members differ in their national or ethnic characteristics and who demonstrate a determination to preserve their culture and heritage. The February 1992 draft, however, contained a separate definition for national and ethnic minorities that expressly designated "Gypsies" as an ethnic but not national minority for the purposes of the Act.[37] The distinction was not merely symbolic given that the array of rights conferred on national minorities, especially in the field of education, exceeded those extended to ethnic minorities. Notably, national minorities' right to learn and use their native languages in "every area of public life" was recognized, in contrast with ethnic minorities, whose right to use native languages was conditioned on "economic, personal and other requirements to be determined by regulation."[38] In addition, the February draft introduced for the first time a taxonomy of national minorities who would fall within the scope of the Act. This taxonomic approach has been criticized as "confusing and self-contradictory,"[39] given that a list of minorities who qualify under the Act is contrary to other provisions of the Bill which state that "national or ethnic self-identity is a basic human right due to individuals and communities alike."[40]

The June 1992 draft contained a compromise solution. The discriminatory national and ethnic distinction with regard to language use

---

[36] Each draft has several versions and so references may vary somewhat.

[37] Article 36 § (2).

[38] Article 9 § (2) and Article 9 § (3).

[39] Csaba Lorincz, "A nemzeti es etnikai kisebbsegi jogok alanyairol," ("On the Subjects of the National and Ethnic Minority Rights"), *Pro Minoritate*, 1992 X-XI at 34-35. *See also Magyar Hirlap*, March 13, April 23, 1992; *Magyar Nemzet*, April 6, 1992; *Nepszabadsag*, February 21, April 18, 1992; *Nepszava*, March 19, 21, April 8, May 28, 1992; *Phralipe*, special edition 1992.

[40] August 1991 draft Ch. I, Article 1. § (2); February 1992 draft Ch. I, Article 2 § (2); June 1992 draft Ch.I, Article 3 § (2).

was deleted and the definitions of ethnic and national minorities conflated into a single one. Article 1 § (2) stated that:

> [f]or the application of this Act, a national or ethnic minority (hereinafter minority) is every group of people indigenous to the territory of Hungary for at least one century which is numerically in the minority among the state's population, whose members are Hungarian citizens and which is distinguished from other members of the population by its own language and culture, heritage, and which manifests awareness of commonality such that it endeavors to preserve this and to express and protect its historically created communal interests.

However, Article 2 retained the taxonomy, listing thirteen indigenous groups which automatically qualify for national and ethnic minority status,[41] though the list is meant to be illustrative rather than limiting:

> "[I]n the event a minority, not listed in [Article] 2. § (1), wishes to ascertain whether it satisfies the conditions contained in [Article] 1, it can submit a petition to the President of Parliament, signed by at least 1,000 Hungarian citizens identifying themselves as members of that minority."[42]

But some critics were not mollified, arguing that the new minority definition was discriminatory, excluding many minorities, especially the Chinese and Vietnamese arriving in Hungary since the mid-1960s, whose numbers exceed those of some of the protected minorities, such as Greeks.

The second main area of controversy in the Minority Bill centered on the problem of minority local governments (or "self-governments"). Following the 1990 elections, Parliament sought to decentralize power by creating territorial units with broad legislative and

---

[41] Bulgarian, Gypsy, Greek, Croatian, Pole, German, Armenian, Romanian, Ukranian, Serb, Slovak, Slovene and Ruthanian.

[42] Article 2 § (2).

17

administrative powers.[43] Although many of the 3,000 "self-governments" had minorities, including Romas, elected to their ranks, the Minority Bill recognized the need for further affirmative measures. Thus the Preamble declared that as self-governments comprise the basis for a democratic system, the creation of minority self-governments is one of the bill's major goals.

The final area of contention was minority representation in Parliament. Article 19 stated that this issue would be regulated by a separate law. In June 1992, the coalition government presented its most recent proposal, according to which each minority group would be required to field a single national list.[44] The first candidate on any list could obtain a seat in Parliament with as few as 3,000 votes, while additional candidates would require some 30,000 votes each to enter Parliament. The proposal envisions an increase in Parliamentary seats by thirteen - one for each of the officially recognized indigenous groups in Hungary. Some minorities, notably Bulgarians, estimated to number fewer than 3,000, may have difficulty in winning even a single mandate. In contrast, Romas may fare well.

As this report was going to press, Helsinki Watch learned that the Law on the Rights of National and Ethnic Minorities was passed by the Hungarian parliament on July 7. Helsinki Watch has not yet received a copy of the law, but has learned that the law defines national and ethnic minorities as

> any group with at least 100 years of residence in Hungary and with its own language and culture. The law stipulates that the choice of identity is voluntary and guarantees the use of names and education in the mother tongue. It declares that minorities have a right to set up their own cultural and heritage organizations including "local and national self-governments," ensuring their cultural autonomy. The law stipulates that a

---

[43] Act LXV 1990.

[44] Hungary's electoral system combines direct representation - individual candidates chosen by a specific electorate - and voting for a national party which then allocates the votes among its internally-picked candidates.

18

"national and ethnic minority fund" be set up within a year to assist the minority self-governments.[45]

Hungary's Romas have benefitted from the legal changes even in the absence of affirmative measures which the Minority Law is expected to confer. In particular, the liberal laws regarding the creation of political, social and cultural associations have led to an unprecedented explosion of Roma organizations. As of mid-1992, some 70 Roma organizations had been registered with the Office of National and Ethnic Minorities; by January 1, 1993, the number had surpassed 100, the majority being regional and local cultural associations. And while the support received from the state, the Office of National Minorities, as well as direct disbursements from Parliament and local self-governments, remains modest,[46] the scale of Roma activities is impressive. Currently there are at least four regularly published Roma journals (*Phralipe, Amaro Drom, Roma Magazin* and Lungo Drom's publications) and Romas are receiving greater airtime for radio and television broadcasting[47] in both Hungarian and Romany. Nevertheless, the mushrooming of Roma associations has proved to be a mixed blessing. As one Roma activist, Attila Muzsar, explained to Helsinki Watch:

> Sure it's a wonderful thing to have all these Roma groups, for the first time I can remember we can finally talk about our identity and issues freely . . . but at the same time with so many parties and associations we spend so much time figuring out who represents whom that we are not taken seriously anymore. And the government knows that, too, and the government wants to divide us Gypsies as much as possible . . . giving

---

[45] *RFE/RL Daily Report,* July 8, 1993, p. 6.

[46] In 1992, the total financial support allocated to Romas for their organizations was only slightly above $1 million. Office of the National and Ethnic Minorities, *in Magyar Hirlap,* July 8, 1992.

[47] Broadcasting on state-run television (TV1 and TV2) has increased from fortnightly to half an hour per week. The future of these broadcasts is uncertain since Parliament has not yet passed a Media Act.

money to one group and not the other is one way to set a wedge between us Romas . . . and, of course, because of all the jealousies, and the fact that no one has any money, we end up being blamed and we blame the other ones as well.

Other changes in the civil law will also have indirect ramifications for the Romas. In light of the growth in racism (see below), Roma advocates are beginning to exploit favorable changes in anti-discrimination laws. In particular, while under the communist regime a plaintiff in any discrimination suit could only be compensated for property damage or loss, or for substantial and lasting physical damage, a recent Constitutional Court decision[48] has held that non-material harm caused by discrimination is also compensable. As a result, tentative steps have now been taken to apply the anti-discrimination laws as a vehicle for suing publishers of racist articles, broadcasts and the like. The future of this form of redress remains unclear, as is its potential implication to chill the freedom of speech.[49]

The efficacy of this remedy is also open to debate: such cases often take years and the damages awarded are primarily symbolic (averaging between $1,000-$3,000). As Marton Rajki, one of the handful of human rights lawyers who have initiated civil suits under this liberalized standard, explained to Helsinki Watch:

It's a long-odds undertaking and this is not America . . . civil rights are still not taken seriously and the judiciary, too, is resistant to awarding non-property damages . . . they often prefer to sit on these cases and so the handful of plaintiffs who try these suits will anyhow lose interest.

Within the area of criminal law, Roma advocates have been pressing hard to convince state officials to send a symbolic message to Hungarian society about the seriousness of anti-Roma violence (see below) by indicting skinheads pursuant to hitherto unused Section 156 of

---

[48] 34/1992 VI. 1 AB.

[49] See appendix for Human Rights Watch Policy Statement on the Protection of "Hate Speech."

the Penal Code which deals with "offenses committed against national, ethnic, racial or religious groups."[50] Finally, in the so-called "great skinhead trial" of 1992, the chief prosecutor decided to indict forty-eight skinheads for violating Section 156. As the Assistant Chief explained to Helsinki Watch:

> As far as I can remember, this skinhead trial was the first time we sought to apply Section 156 . . . we looked hard at all those cases where racism is charged and frankly often we could find nothing definite . . . in this case, though, the racial or anti-ethnic bias was clear and the use of the anti-ethnic provision was compelling.

But this "pioneering" effort ultimately failed as the Court of the Capital City modified the charges to the routinely applied combined offenses of hooliganism, breach of peace and slander[51] and, in November 1992, two defendants were placed on one-year probation, 37 received suspended sentences and nine were sentenced to short prison terms.[52] The judge's refusal to apply Section 156 is currently being appealed.

Ability to exercise rights

In spite of the constitutional prohibition of discrimination on the basis of race, color, gender, language, religion, creed, national origin or social position, property or birth place,[53] Romas face considerable difficulties in enforcing their rights. Although some forms of discrimination, such as the passage of "ghetto laws" imposing night-to-

---

[50] Penal Code 156 § states that "[a] person causing grievous bodily or spiritual harm to another for belonging to a national, ethnic, racial or religious group commits a criminal offense punishable by between two and eight years of incarceration."

[51] Sections 271 and 179 respectively of the Penal Code.

[52] *Beszelo*, December 5, 1992.

[53] Article 70/A § (1).

dawn curfews of Roma inhabitants of villages, are extremely rare,[54] Helsinki Watch has collected numerous reports of other types of discrimination or exclusion from public and private services. The majority of public sector complaints focus on the second-class treatment meted out by self-governments (minority local governments) in dealing with Romas. Restricted access to private facilities, especially bars, restaurants and discos is another recurring grievance, as well as allegations of discrimination in hiring and firing from workplaces.

Access to privately owned bars, restaurants and discos varies greatly, not simply from county to county, but also from one village to another, depending on the attitude of the public officials, the degree of Roma integration, the extent of Roma organization and, increasingly, the role of Catholic and Protestant clerics. As Gabor Noszkai, a civil rights lawyer, summed up to Helsinki Watch:

> It's not unheard of to have one village with perfectly good relations between Gypsies and Magyars with no problem of mixing in the pubs while a few kilometers away in the next village's pub you'd find a "no Gypsies wanted" policy in effect.

While precise information is not available, anecdotal evidence suggests that institutionalized exclusion of Romas from pubs is the exception rather than the rule. However, covert discrimination - ranging from refusal to serve Roma customers, often without any explanation, to inflating prices so as to discourage Romas from attending the establishments - is widespread. Incidents of these types have been reported to Helsinki Watch from several regions and settlements of varying sizes, from villages (e.g. Tiszabo, Kevermes) to towns (Kalocsa, Mohacs, Ozd) and cities (Budapest, Eger, Miskolc, Salgotarjan and Tatabanya) suggesting that these practices, official denials notwitstanding,

---

[54] One such documented case occurred in the village of Het in 1991, where the mayor imposed an 8 p.m. curfew on a Roma family and denied the family access to the pub, grocery store and other places selling alcohol. Information is from an article by Gyorgy Kobanyai, journalist, from Roma Parliament.

are common.[55] As one youth in his twenties commented to Helsinki Watch:[56]

> Those who say discrimination does not exist are fools or liars. We know exactly that it's not safe to go to a number of pubs and discos, and not just ones where skinheads go. Sometimes people look at you and there is no mistaking what they want you to do . . . but most times they aren't even that "kind" but tell you straight out that as a stinking gypsy you should get lost before they call the cops.

Roma leaders also maintain that discriminatory practices pervade daily life in countless other ways, ranging from problems faced in transportation, such as taxi drivers' refusals to pick up Roma passengers, to exclusion from community activities. One recurrent complaint, for example, is local councils' refusals to admit Romas into the Civil Guards (Polgarorseg), a voluntary patrol force organized by residents.[57] This discriminatory practice is rooted in bigotry, as in many villages it is assumed that Romas, with few exceptions, are all actual or potential criminals.[58]

But while these discriminatory practices undoubtedly occur, their magnitude is almost impossible to estimate. Labor market discrimination, for instance, has not been systematically studied, while anecdotal

---

[55] Helsinki Watch received such reports concerning some two dozen settlements, either from human rights activists or from published sources including the Raoul Wallenberg Circle, Office of Mayor, Budapest, Office of National and Ethnic Minorities and Ottilia Solt, MP (SZDSZ). Police officials contacted by Helsinki Watch denied that discrimination exists (Ibolya Orbai ORFK [National Police Headquarters] January 13, 1993), as did Janos Fabian, Assis. Chief Pros., Budapest (interview January 13, 1993) ("I'm convinced that there is no discrimination in Hungary").

[56] Interview with "Sanyi" M., Budapest, January 16, 1993.

[57] *See, e.g., Amaro Drom* No. 11, March 6, 1992, at 4-5.

[58] Helsinki Watch interview with Gyula Naday, President, Magyar Ciganyok Demokrata Szovetsege, January 12, 1993.

information remains perfunctory and ambiguous. Still, given that Roma unemployment, on average, is five times that of the non-Roma population, discrimination appears to be a significant factor. As one sociologist commented:

> The structural changes and streamlining has in many places become the perfect excuse to "degypsify" the workplace.[59]

One area in which anti-Roma discrimination can easily be detected is housing. Not only does the housing condition of Hungary's Romas remain uniformly inferior to that of the non-Roma population (see above) but Romas experience considerable obstacles in gaining access to the limited housing stocks which are distributed by local councils. Jozsef R. recounted to Helsinki Watch the story of his son's futile efforts to obtain council housing in the city of Miskolc:

> We've been living three generations, thirteen of us in this apartment [one small room and an eat-in kitchen with a closet, the apartment measuring no more than 300 square feet - ed.] for nearly twenty years . . . well, as things became impossible, you know, the sons wanted privacy with their wives and to raise a family - which they could not do here, with the space we have they had to live in the kitchen closet . . . so over the years I managed to get my two eldest out into a decent enough place . . . which wasn't easy but thank God we had a Gypsy in the local council and he helped us . . . but now my youngest who got too impatient for his own good, had enough of waiting three years for his place, so he goes off to the council and signs some paper without even reading it . . . no surprise, they anyhow think we're a bunch of stupid no-gooders . . . so my son gets a house - if you would call that rat-hole a house - which has no windows, no door, no heating, no running water, no nothing . . . and to make things worse the paper my stupid son signed says that if we don't pay the 30,000

---

[59] Roma Parliament: "Situation Assessment" (manuscript).

forint [some $400] to fix everything up within three weeks, he'll be taken off the waiting list with prejudice!

As Erno Kalo, the local Phralipe representative, explained to Helsinki Watch, this family's plight was far from unusual:

> There are some decent people at the housing agency, but even they are tempted to screw the Gypsy. The number of times they have done this to Gypsies I know, try to fob off places they would not allow their animals to stay in . . . if you think it's unusual that they ended up with a house with nothing in it you're mistaken -there are dozens of pigsties which non-Gypsies would not touch but the council knows we're desperate enough to take. And, this has also happened, once we Gypsies fix up the place we get kicked out . . . I'm not saying that's always the case, but that has happened . . . and now because of this boy's stupidity we'll have to fight the council weeks just to put him back on the top of the list where he belongs.

Roma leaders believe, and human rights activists concur, that abuses of procedural law by self-governments to the detriment of Roma citizens are not isolated occurrences. As Szabolcs Bognar[60] explains:

> The problem is that passing laws is one thing and enforcing them is quite another. While the legal framework of the country is quite good, the same cannot be said of our legal culture . . . we're given constitutional rights but we haven't really learned what the rule of law really entails . . . rights and democracy are all fine but amidst the mounting social and economic stress people want to bend the rules . . . so administrators don't always play by the book if they see no compelling reason to . . . and Gypsies are often the victims. For instance, if a local administrator does not want to be pestered with repeated appeals against a fine or a penalty, let's say, he

---

[60] Director, Office of Social Policy, Office of Mayor, Budapest. Helsinki Watch interview, January 15, 1993.

will simply ante-date the notice so by the time it's delivered the time for appeal has already expired . . . and there are many other practices which, when combined, may make the Gypsy's ability to get his dues very difficult.

Romas relate other forms of discrete discriminatory practices and abuses of power, ranging from delaying or withholding Romas' social entitlements to threatening to withdraw their children's educational grants or health benefits. Roma advocates also point out that abuses are not only hard to detect but remain difficult to redress. Without minority ombudsmen, another constitutionally mandated requirement which remains unfulfilled in the absence of a minority law,[61] and a paucity of well-qualified social workers, lawyers and human rights activists, only the most egregious abuses can be tackled. As Bea Morvai, a case worker with SZETA in Budapest, explained to Helsinki Watch:

> When the local council decided last year [1991] to throw out a pregnant Gypsy woman with two small kids onto the street, in the middle of winter on the day before Christmas, that was sufficiently bloodcurdling to have the newspapers show some interest and so the council relented . . . but when a council does something less spectacular - say shuts off gas and electricity without the resident having had the chance to proceed with the administrative appeals - who will listen then? Nobody.

The ability of Romas to seek redress for violations varies from place to place. In most urban centers, such as Budapest, Miskolc and Szolnok, Roma associations (e.g., Phralipe, Lungo Drom) are well organized. In addition, in Budapest, for instance, the VIIIth district[62] with a large Roma population has set up its own minority self-

---

[61] Constitution, Chapter 5, Article 32/B §§ (1)-(7).

[62] Budapest is divided into twenty-two districts or local councils.

government and appointed its own ombudsman, as have several other local councils throughout the country.[63]

Recourse to the judiciary for vindication of Roma rights is not viewed as a viable alternative because it is too expensive and painstakingly slow. Nor are Roma leaders confident that political alliances forged on the national level are of great benefit in battling local abuses. Thus, while the party of the Free Democrats is generally perceived as the most progressive party on Roma issues on the national level, so much so that it has two Roma members of parliament among its ranks,[64] Free Democrat mayors and self-government representatives do not necessarily share this progressive creed. As Bea Morvai sums up:

> Perhaps, on the whole, SZDSZ self-governments lean more toward the Gypsies, but I would not be adamant on that point . . . and truth be known we have had a good number of complaints about many SZDSZ mayors as well.

Relations with police and the criminal justice system

Prior to the assimilationist drive of 1961, Romas were subjected to institutionalized discrimination, compelled to carry identity cards recording them as Gypsies. This practice was discontinued in the 1960s, but the Kadar regime retained other oppressive legal measures, tolerated systematic abuses and violations of the criminal procedures, and created new discriminatory devices. Harassment by the police, ranging from constant ID checks to arbitrary arrests, was routine, beatings during interrogations were frequent and occasionally the "anti-terror" units were

---

[63] *e.g.*, Kecskemet.

[64] see above; The Young Democrats (Fidesz) and the Socialists (MSZP) are also generally perceived - by Romas and non-Romas alike, as gauged by opinion polls - to be receptive to Roma needs. In contrast the governing coalition and its constituent parties, especially the Democratic Forum (MDF) and the Independent Smallholders (FKgP) are perceived, for reasons discussed below, as very hostile to Romas in general.

thrown in to "discipline" the local Roma population.[65] Legal methods of control included police supervision" (the so-called "ref," or rendorfelugyelet) which could impose dusk-to-dawn curfews on convicted felons. "Gypsies," together with vagrants and dangerous felons, were constantly seen as a threat to society.[66]

In addition, a special "department for miscellaneous crimes" was established in Budapest in the 1970s for studying "Gypsy modes of criminality." This pseudo-scientific enterprise involved, among others, the collection of some 2,000 Roma fingerprints, for the most part belonging to juveniles in state institutions without criminal records, to find out whether or not Gypsies' genetic propensity for criminality could be detected from their dermatoglyphics.[67] Although this patently racist undertaking was abandoned, the department was dissolved in 1990 and the police pledged to abandon classification of criminals by racial/ethnic origin or putatively racial/ethnic *modus operandi*,[68] police officials continue to use "gypsy criminality" as a term of art.[69] As one senior criminal investigator commented:

> I cannot accept why I should not say that there exists
> gypsy criminality, when, for example, the expressions
> gypsy music and gypsy folklore are acceptable. But I

---

[65] Interview with Gabor Ivanyi by *168 Ora*, May 19, 1992; Helsinki Watch interviews with Ottilia Solt (January 5, 1993), Janos Ladanyi (January 4, 1993), Aladar Horvath (January 6, 1993), Gyula Naday (January 12, 1993) and Zsolt Csalog (January 5 and 12, 1993).

[66] Police memorandum from the 1970s cited by *Magyar Hirlap*, March 14, 1992.

[67] Gabor Noszkai, "Ciganysag es Rendorseg" ("Gyspies and the Police"), manuscript at 3; *Belugyi Szemle*, June 1987, at 15.

[68] The pledge was made on December 21, 1991 by Andras Turos, director of the Hungarian Police (ORFK) and then deputy Minister of Interior. Cited from Gabor Noszkai *op. cit.*, at 4 and *Magyar Nemzet*, December 22, 1989.

[69] Gabor Noszkai, *op. cit.* at 4-5.

hasten to add: I use the word only for differentiating among techniques.[70]

Moreover, there appears to be a broadly shared sentiment among ranks of the police and the population that these departments should be reinstituted. This view of law enforcement officials was summed up in a 1991 interview with Gyula Borgulya, a member of the dissolved unit.[71] Mr. Borgulya stated that:

> Eighty percent of violent crimes are committed by Gypsies, you can't deny it, this is a fact . . . [p]eople tend to misunderstand what we say about Gypsy crimes. By this we simply refer to Gypsies' methods of committing crimes as opposed to non-Gypsies . . . [i]t is a pity that we are not allowed to differentiate between Gypsies and other individuals, we have to combat them in the same way with the same means, nevertheless they cause us much more problems. It should be recognized that in the interest of the whole society such differentiation is justified and all competent authorities should have one or two experts on the Gypsy problem, this would make our job a lot easier.

Though Mr. Borgulya insisted that he was no bigot, his comments left no doubt as to his racist views as he proceeded to explain that:

> Gypsy burglars ravage. They hate people who possess something and they want to destroy what they can't take away. Because of the extreme nervousness they often leave a piece of excrement on the spot. The detective must take it to the lab, the analysis gives evidence of the burglar's blood group, what he has eaten, etc.

While Mr. Borgulya was officially reprimanded for airing his opinions, which also included the recommendation for "Magyars" to

---

[70] Laszlo Tonhauser *in Heti Vilaggazdasag Portre*, January 16, 1993.

[71] *Pesti Hirlap*, Oct. 30-31, 1991; letters *Pesti Hirlap* November 1 and 5, 1991.

protect themselves by the use of illegal gas-sprays, following a call for sanctions by civil right activists and the Office of National and Ethnic Minorities, a number of police officials speaking to Helsinki Watch on condition of anonymity voiced their agreement with Mr. Borgulya's assessment of the "Gypsy criminality."

Human right activists point out that such negative perceptions about the Romas are widespread (see below) despite any reliable evidence to support these views. On the contrary, the few studies conducted over the past decade dealing with "Gypsy criminality" reveal a different picture. One such study undertaken in 1982, which did support the retention of the special police department for "Gypsy offenses," concluded that while crime by Romas is twice that of the national average, and that among a certain segment of Romas crime has become a lifestyle, less than 1.5 percent of the Roma population committed criminal offenses. The most recent detailed study, based on a survey with prisoners, concludes that criminal behavior in mostly Roma-inhabited areas is not higher than such behavior in poor areas inhabited predominantly by non-Romas - implying that the major factor in criminal offenses is poverty.[72]

Widespread anti-Roma attitudes have led to Roma mistrust of the police. "I don't trust the police. They are afraid of the Gypsies and they rather permit the skinheads to beat the Gypsies," said one Roma in a recent interview.[73] "The police treat us all as criminals anyway, so there is no point asking them for help," another young Roma commented to Helsinki Watch. Others voiced fear that the local police would hold them collectively accountable for the behavior of individual Romas. In one village where an old man was beaten by an unknown assailant, the police allegedly threatened that if the old man were to die, all the Gypsies would

---

[72] Istvan Tauber and Katalin Veg, "A ciganysag bunozesenek nehany osszefugese," (Some interrelationships of Gypsy criminality"), 29 *Magyar Jog*, No. 8, August; Janos Ladanyi, "Szabdsagvesztes-Buntetesuket Toltok Lakohelyeinek Terbeni Elhelyezkedese Budapesten" ("Residential Segregation of Imprisoned Offenders in Budapest"), *Ter es Tarsadalom* 1991 #4 at 17-35.

[73] *168 Ora*, November 24, 1992 at 4.

be subjected to the same fate. "Your lives won't be worth that of a dog," the Romas were told.[74]

Although verbal threats and racial insults appear to be widespread, thus discouraging many Romas from asking the police for assistance, those who do seek help do not necessarily obtain it. Recriminations about police reluctance to intervene when Romas are assailed have been surfacing ever since September 1990, when some 150 skinheads launched a pogrom-like attack on a Roma-populated section of the town of Eger. The police arrived only some four hours into the attack, did not notify their superior officers and failed to seek reinforcement for three days even though the town was gripped by hysteria as the victimized Romas began to strike back (by beating up some locals mistakenly identified as skinheads).[75]

The reason for the attack as well as the police failure to intervene in a timely fashion has never been properly accounted for; some civil right activists suggest that non-intervention was deliberate,[76] a charge denied by police officials who point to different factors. As Janos Bodracska, chief of the Budapest police force recently commented: "[t]ruth is we're waiting for the police law, which we badly need . . . we're working with regulations, half of which are outdated and we don't know what proper criminal procedures ought to be."[77] Others point out that the creation of civil guards, a volunteer organization made up of locals to patrol neighborhoods, has created problems of command and co-ordination for the police as these units are financed by the local self-

---

[74] Cited from transcript of complaint recorded regarding the events in Tarnazsadany, October 1, 1992.

[75] *Beszelo*, September 26, 1992; Helsinki Watch interview with Janos Ladanyi, January 4, 1993.

[76] *E.g.*, Helsinki Watch interviews with Janos Ladanyi, January 4, 1993, Zsolt Csalog, January 5, 1993.

[77] Statement made on June 25, 1992; cited in, Vannek-e Emberi Jogaik, A szinesboru diakok helyzete a fovarosban es a skinhead jelenseg ("Do they have human rights?, The Situation of Colored Students in the Capital City and the Skinhead Phenomenon," Committee of Minorities, Human Rights and Religious Affairs, Self-Government of the Budapest Capital City (hereinafter: *White Book*) at 94.

government and are accountable to the mayor and not the local police official. As Ottilia Solt explains:

> The country is filled with discharged militiamen, soldiers, police and thousands of frustrated and angry men who are forced into retirement because of the economic and political changes . . . these people form a large potential source for the PO ["polgarorseg" i.e. the civil guard] . . . while they are not allowed to carry weapons and their task is supposed to be limited to contacting the police, if problems erupt they often prefer to handle the matters themselves . . . they almost always carry sticks, occasionally spray-guns and even if the police, which in smaller villages means a solitary policeman, if at all, wanted to control them there would not be much he could do.

Although human rights advocates acknowledge that lack of training and absence of clear procedural guidelines may be a factor, they insist that police non-intervention has become too frequent to be so easily dismissed. While Roma allegations have not been systematically tallied, Helsinki Watch received numerous reports that such police inaction is common. As Gabor Noszkai told Helsinki Watch:

> Attacks on Gypsies generally receive low priority. If the "trouble" does not seem to develop into a large-scale brawl the police probably tend to ignore it . . . but, these matters are obviously difficult to prove and the vast majority of Gypsies left helpless would not even contemplate complaining to the authorities . . . which means that no-one knows the real magnitude of this problem.[78]

These claims are buttressed by the better documented police non-intervention with respect to the approximately 3,000 foreign students - mostly African, Middle Eastern and Asians - who have been increasingly

---

[78] Helsinki Watch inteview, January 16, 1993.

targeted by skinheads.[79] According to the Martin Luther King (MLK) Association, founded in 1991 on behalf of foreign students, there were some ninety skinhead attacks between January 1991 and April 1992. The police, on the scene on fewer than a dozen occasions, refused to intervene on three occasions, once arrested the victim and on at least one other occasion reportedly beat up the victims. On two further occasions the police delayed or outright refused to register the complaint.[80]

Roma leaders also complain that even when the police move against the skinheads they get deferential treatment. As one Roma complained to Helsinki Watch:

> Hatred of Gypsies runs deep with the police; if skinheads were less public in persecuting us the police would be glad not to intervene. . . as it is they get arrested less and don't go to court as often as would be the case if a Gypsy beat a Magyar.

But even when the police take measures, Roma leaders point to the bias and deferential treatment afforded to the skinheads. In particular, Romas interviewed by Helsinki Watch were uniformly

---

[79] The 3,000 figure is from the *White Book*; elsewhere the number of foreign students is estimated to have been closer to 4,000 (*Beszelo*, November 14, 1992).

[80] The total number of attacks (almost all by skinheads) on foreign students is from the *White Book* (supra) and Marton Ill, Gabor Noszkai and Janos Zolnay, "Koznapi Esemenyek Kronikaja," ("Chronicle of Everyday Events"), manuscript compiled by Raoul Wallenberg Association, December, 1992. Only in seven instances does the record indicate police presence. Refusals to intervene were recorded on January 17, 1992 (attack on two African and one Latin American students at Deak square), April 20, 1992 (attack on two African students at Ors Vezer Square - allegedly several police refused to intervene), May 9, 1992 (nine Sudanese students attacked by 25 skinheads at the Globe disco); September 11, 1992 (Nigerian student attacked at Eastern railway station and is arrested by police); April 24, 1992 (two Kenyan students attacked and police refused to register complaint), August 16, 1992 the President of the Mayor's Office of Human Rights comes to the aid of a Sierra Leone student attacked by two skinheads, but police refuses to register complaint for several hours (officer subsequently disciplined); November 12, 1991 (two policemen beat up black students).

incensed at the decision of Janos Bodracska, Chief of the Budapest police, to invite eighteen skinheads for a meeting on September 4, 1992, in which the Chief sought to dissuade them from carrying out further attacks - while voicing his agreement with the skinheads that there are too many foreigners in Hungary. As Gabor Demszky, mayor of Budapest, explained to Helsinki Watch:

> Bodracska's meeting with the skinheads was an enormous mistake for it played into the hands of those who want to see the movement legitimized. Measures such as this can only help this marginal phenomenon to become more respectable, and thereby larger.

Yet, critics also emphasize that the police force itself is divided on what approach to take, and several Roma leaders and human rights advocates voiced their support for Antal Kacziba, Chief of the Criminal Division of the National Police force, who publicly opposed Bodracska's policy and sought a tougher stance against the skinheads.[81]

Romas also complain that the police often go beyond denying assistance and that they frequently harass and physically assault them during routine driver's license checks, as well as in public places such as railway and bus stations and pubs, often with rubber baton and on several occasion by the use of mace guns.[82] Others assert that the police view Romas as the natural suspects in virtually all crimes occurring locally and that they are often beaten in order to get confessions.

---

[81] On Antal Kacziba's call for tougher stance: *Nepszabadsag*, September 5, 1992; on Janos Bodracska's meeting, *id*. On Antal Kacziba's opposition: *Magyar Hirlap*, September 9, 1992.

[82] The most recent such episode, somewhat unusual in that the victim did file an official complaint, occurred on November 27, 1992 in Szendro, B.A.Z., where three policemen used both rubber batons and mace to discipline local Romas after an altercation in a local pub. Another incident, this one well-publicized, occurred in Marceli where police allegedly used excessive force during an ID check in a local pub. ("Remalom Marceliban," ("Nightmare in Marceli") *Kurir*, October 2, 1992).

Here, in Kevermes, they can easily beat a man to death. Whoever comes to the village the locals will say that we steal, cheat. In this county, in fact, things like breaking in through the roof to elderly people, tying them up and robbing them have also been taking place. And this is blamed on us, the Gypsies. For this, the police are beating us. There was a burglary at the post office once, and all of us [there are some 270 Romas in that settlement] were taken to the police station. They beat us all though we saw and heard nothing.[83]

Roma leaders claim such abuses are widespread while police officials maintain that these practices do not exist at all. Official denials notwithstanding, it is evident that these and similar abuses exist and that Romas fall victims to a disproportionate extent to police abuses.[84]

Helsinki Watch also received reports that police have conducted large-scale police raids, including by special commando units, against local Roma populations. The circumstances and nature of these police commando raids vary. One raid, at Nyirtabor, on March 18, 1992, for instance - comprised of a special action group with ten men, ten civil guards, three detectives and forty-three regular police - was precipitated by events spanning two weeks. On March 6, a dying Roma man was discovered on the edge of the Roma shanty-town; locals believed he was a victim of a skinhead attack. The police and an ambulance was called but did not arrive for hours. By that time the man had died. Although initially some detectives announced that skinheads were the probable cause of the deadly assault, subsequently the official position changed to an attack by a stray dog. Locals, however, were not convinced and the rumor began to circulate that more skinhead attacks were imminent.

---

[83] Gusztav Nagy, "Kevermes, ahol mindenki fel" ("Kevermes, where everyone is afraid"), *Amaro Drom*, 1992/23 at 8-11. The local police chief rejected the allegations that he personally assaulted anyone but did admit that "it's true, when they kick up a row with cars without a driver's license, then I have to step in." In the village Roma-police tensions were probably exacerbated by the fact that the local police chief had been attacked three years before by a Roma who has not yet been charged with the offense.

[84] *See also Beszelo*, March 6, 1993, which shares this assessment.

Amidst this atmosphere of panic, a police patrol with one regular police officer and two civil guards was attacked by some fifteen Romas who believed that the dreaded skinhead attack was about to begin. It was in response to this attack that the commando action was undertaken.

During the raid, the police ordered everyone out of their houses and conducted a search of all premises, lasting some four hours. While the police were expressly ordered not to harm anyone, sporadic assaults - in one instance with a rubber baton - did take place. There has not been any subsequent investigation of the legality of the commando raid and alleged use of excessive force.[85]

In another large scale police raid, apparently prompted by local officials' request for a show of force to discipline "trouble-makers," police anti-terror units swept through Vasarosnameny, Aranyosapati and Gyure (Szabolcs-Szatmar-Bereg county) on February 7, 1992, during the course of which some ten Romas were seriously beaten. At least one woman, the wife of a Roma beaten in the course of his arrest, was attacked by a specially-trained police dog. The mayor of Aranyosapati thanked the police for their "forceful handling of the matter" and the Minister of the Interior dismissed criticisms of the raid:

> It was I who drafted the directive that 1992 would be the year of accountability . . . I am convinced that I must proceed correctly, in accordance with this, if I don't wish to reproach the police who fulfil their duty and I shake their hands.[86]

In one village,[87] home to over 2,000 including some 300 Romas, the local policeman admitted to having participated in a recent raid

---

[85] The account and quote by the eyewitness is from Janos Pelle, "Borfejuek, polgarorok, kommandosok," *Amaro Drom*, November 1992, at 4-7.

[86] Reports are from *Amaro Drom*, November 1992 at 8; *Beszelo*, September 26, 1992 at 8; *168 Ora*, May 19, 1992; Minister's statement is from the Minutes of Parliament, May 26, 1992 at 17621-17625, reprinted in Raoul Wallenberg chronicle op. cit. at 2.

[87] The local policeman spoke on the condition that neither his name, nor that of the village which would reveal his identity, be used.

against Romas organized in conjunction with his superiors from the nearby town. He claimed that violent and petty crime alike have been rising in the past year and that the locals were becoming fed up with the Romas whom they held responsible for the attacks.

> There are some decent ones among them who live just like I do or anyone else, but they are very few. There are two or three families that are very good but there are only some twenty-eight people who keep the 400 alive. The majority of these Gypsies never worked - not even when it was called shirking,[88] not now when it's called unemployment . . . many of them also made trouble . . . there were two or three families . . . and by a family I mean fifty or sixty people . . . and they were beating and literally killing one another . . . now we have twenty-three Gypsies in the local jail awaiting trial for everything from burglary to theft to attempted murder . . . and the problem is many are still at large . . . I can only catch them but often they are back here before I get home . . . and this is what makes the locals angry.

The policeman claimed that locals were scared, oftentimes not willing to lodge formal complaints against Romas for fear of retribution, and angry at the law's inability to stop the crime. In the past the villagers occasionally took matters into their own hands. He described one such incident when half a dozen villagers donned Ku Klux Klan outfits and attacked Roma houses.

> That worked . . . the Gypsies were terrified for a while . . . but this is not a solution either . . . Now we have the civil guard and they are a lot of help . . .but here, in a village such as Ny to maintain the peace by using only legal means is absolutely impossible . . . here if I find an offender he laughs in my face [saying] that he did nothing. And if one listens carefully enough, it's for sure he'll tell you everything he did, where and how, with how

---

[88] This is a reference to "work-avoidance" which was a criminal offense during the Communist regime.

many of them, where they took the staff . . . but this is no good for me for I'll be denounced for abuse of power and forced confession. It won't matter that I stopped the crime, I am the one who won't get holiday pay and promotion . . . but the village doesn't want to see that this is how it is and they say "if we find them beat them" and "give back the police power," "give back the 'ref'" and "give free reign to the police" . . . but these things are now impossible.

The policeman complained that with the most effective method, the dawn-to-dusk curfew (the "ref") no longer available to him, he felt he had no alternative but to participate in the locally organized "commando" unit which consisted of police and numerous civilians as well, many of whom also used rubber batons and mace guns. The policeman readily admitted that the purpose of the raid was to beat up a few dozen or so of the "Gypsy trouble-raisers":

It was a little discipline-making exercise undertaken in Ny on two occasions. . . it had an incredible impact, for the Gypsies were so scared that they did not dare to leave their homes for two weeks. Really, they stood guarding their homes too scared to go into the street . . . but now a disciplinary action has begun against the unit.[89]

Other reliable reports of either police-organized raids or police-abetted vigilante attacks, usually by the civil guards, have been received from most counties with large Roma populations (Szabolcs-Szatmar-Berege, Borsod-Abauj-Zemplen, Nograd, Becs-Kiskun and Jasz-Nagykun-Szolnok) with some of the specific sites of such attacks including Aszod (November 1991), Pomaz (November 1992), Kazincbarcika (February 1991), Nagyborzsony (June 1991), Putnok (August and September 1990, fall of 1991), Vasarosnameny, Aranyosapati and Gyure (February 1992),

---

[89] At the time of the interview, the policeman's superior was suspended. Helsinki Watch has no further information on the status of the proceedings.

Nyirtabor (March 1992), Tarcal (December 1991) and Tarnazsadas (October 1992).[90]

Human rights advocates also argue that recently adopted changes in the Penal Code[91] discriminate against or impose a disparate impact on Romas. In particular, under the new procedures, those indicted without a permanent workplace and residence would not be released on bail, nor would they have an opportunity to see an attorney until the day of their trial.[92] Furthermore, conditions in many pre-trial detention centers violate domestically and internationally-mandated minimum standards as detainees are often held in overcrowded cells, frequently with no heat in winter time or running water in summer, giving rise to illness and infectious diseases.[93] Thus Romas, who on average are much more likely to be unemployed and detained than non-Romas, are clearly victimized by these procedures.

Public opinion and the press

Prejudice against Romas is not a novel phenomenon in Hungarian society. While overt manifestation of such prejudice was not tolerated during the Kadar regime it surfaced in the everyday use of language - as "Gypsy" became a shorthand for a bundle of undesirable attributes, ranging from deviance to criminal or immoral behavior. Public opinion surveys conducted in the 1970s also confirmed that prejudices remained and resisted the Communist Party's integration policy. One large survey conducted in the mid 70s, for instance, revealed that more than one quarter of Hungarians thought of Romas as lazy, immoral and

---

[90] *Amaro Drom*, November 1992; *Beszelo*, September 26, 1992; Helsinki Watch interviews with Janos Ladanyi, Ottilia Solt, Zsolt Csalog, Gabor Noszkai and Aladar Horvath.

[91] Enacted in 1993 March.

[92] From Gabor Noszkai "Ciganysag es Rendorseg" *op. cit.* at 7.

[93] *Rendeszeti Szemle*, January 1993, at 3-16.

prone to criminal behavior.[94]   Other studies showed that many Hungarians viewed Romas as "work-shy" and welfare parasites who receive too many social benefits.

Recent studies indicate that these prejudices are intensifying. A 1989 study found that more than half of Hungarians think Romas receive too many benefits, and support for positive discrimination (affirmative action) has fallen dramatically; while in 1978 one in two supported subsidized housing for Romas, by 1989 the level of support had fallen to one in eight. While in 1978, one third of those who responded favored residential segregation, by 1989, the response rose to almost two thirds. Two thirds of the respondents in the 1989 survey wanted to see a tougher police stance against Romas and one-third voiced support for a policy of forced repatriation to India.[95] A recent survey found that 79 percent of Hungarians hate the Romas[96] while another indicated that some 10 percent of the population would like to see Romas exterminated.[97]

But with the newly found political freedoms, the anti-Roma (as well as anti-immigrant and anti-Semitic) sentiments need no longer be confined to whispers. Since 1990, there has been an explosion of the public display of racism, ranging from graffiti to verbal and published expressions. While two years ago overtly fascist graffiti such as "kill the

---

[94] Endre Hann, Egy Remhir Nyomaban. Esettanulmany. (*Pursuit of a Rumor. A Case Study*). Results reported in David Crowe op. cit. at 304.

[95] Miklos Tomka, "Gazdasagi valtozas es a ciganysaggal kapcsolatos kozvelemeny," ("Economic change and popular opinion concerning the Gypsies,") in Agnes Utasi and Agned Meszaros (eds.) op. cit. 8-36.

[96] *Beszelo*, October 12, 1991 at 21; the opinion study also showed that 40 percent of Hungarians hated Hungarians arriving from Romania and that Romanians and Jews were despised by 30 percent and 11 percent of the population respectively. The survey, conducted by The Times Mirror Centre of the USA, also found that Romas were hated by 91 percent of the population of (then) Czechoslovakia, 71 percent of Bulgarians, 59 percent of Germans and 50 percent among the Spaniards.

[97] Helsinki Watch interview with Marta Pankucsi, January 7, 1993.

Gypsy" were considered "relatively rare,"[98] today graffiti bearing messages such as "Gypsy-free zone," "a good Gypsy is a dead Gypsy," as well as walls dubbed with swastikas may be seen in virtually every town.

Skinheads, neo-Nazis and fascist organizations are also publishing and distributing a growing number of magazines and newsletters specializing in Holocaust revisionism and discussing ethnic cleansing and impending race wars. The neo-Nazi National Socialist Action Group (recently renamed Hungarian National Profile), headquartered in the industrial city of Gyor and linked with other Nazi organizations in Austria, Germany and the USA has its own organ, *Uj Rend* (*New Order*), while its homespun equivalent - self-proclaimed heirs of the Hungarian Arrow Cross - the party which under Ferenc Szalasi, installed by Hitler in 1944, slaughtered and deported hundreds of thousands of Jews and several thousand Romas - distributes leaflets.

Skinheads, in turn, distribute *Kitartas!* (*Perseverance!*), published in Germany and the locally-produced *Pannonbulldog*. Other extreme ring-wing publications whose repertoire also consists of anti-Roma, as well as anti-Semitic and anti-foreigner diatribes and Holocaust revisionism include *Hunnia* and *Szittya Kurt*.[99] *Szent Korona* (*Sacred Crown*), another outright fascist journal, has now ceased publication. The paper has been charged with the "crime of incitement against the community and offense to a person of authority" and its editor, Laszlo Rohmanyi, leader of the Kereszteny Nemzeti Unio (Christian National Union or KNU) who is currently on trial as an accessory to murder, received a six months suspended sentence.[100]

In addition to more or less regular publications, most of the skinhead and fascist organizations also print and distribute leaflets inciting hatred. In one recent episode, for instance, posters bearing

---

[98] Peter T. Zselensky, "Apartheid magyar modra," ("Apartheid in the Hungarian Way") *Phralipe* 1991 No. 10 at 20-21.

[99] Sources on skinheads and neo-Nazis include: *White Book* infra; *Nepszabdsag*, November 28, 1992, December 7, 1992; *168 Ora*, November 24, 1992; *Heti Vilag Gazdasag*, January 2, 1993 at 55-57; *Pro Minoritate*, 1992 X-XI at 5 and interviews with Zoltan Gal, journalist.

[100] On the incitement charge and sentence, Hungarian Radio, Budapest 1300 gmt 8 Feb 93. On murder trial *Magyar Hirlap*, January 13, 1993 at 5.

swastikas and the slogan "out with foreigners" were plastered around Budapest's Castle District.[101]

Extremists elements do not limit their expression of hate to printed materials. There are now several skinhead groups playing the so-called "oi" music (e.g. Pannonskins, CPG, Oi-kor (Oi-era), Mos-oi (Oi-smile), ZEF and Egeszseges Fejbor (Healthy Headskin)) and their lyrics invariably deal with themes such as the destruction of "Blacks, Gypsies, Arabs and Jews," other unwanted "foreigners" and communists. The lyrics of CPG (an acronym for Cigany Pusztito Garda, or Gypsy Extermination Guard)[102] and Mos-oi in particular are regarded as the "skinhead bible." This "bible" includes text such as the following:

> The flamethrower is the only weapon I need to win,
> All Gypsy adults and children we'll exterminate,
> But we can kill all of them at once in unison,
> When it's done we can advertise: Gypsy-Free Zone
>
> (Gypsy-Free-Zone)

> We'll get rid of everyone whom we don't need
> Including the garbage immigrants.
> The immigrants' wage can only be death
> We'll have to chase away all of the Blacks.
> For the Arabs machine guns await
> Above Palestine atom clouds gather.
>
> (Immigrant's wages)[103]

---

[101] MTI (Hungarian Telegraphic Agency) report January 25, 1993.

[102] CPG may have initially stood for "Coitus Punk Group;" nowadays, however, it is universally known to designate Cigany Pusztito Garda.

[103] See also Paul Hockenos, "Racism Unbound in the Land of the Magyars," *New Politics*, Vol. IV, No. 2, 1993 Winter 69, 75.

Skinheads and extreme right-wing organizations[104] occasionally don Nazi uniforms and, in the case of skinheads, decorate their own uniforms with Nazi and Hungarian fascist insignias. These symbols are prominently displayed especially during football (soccer) matches. Almost all major football teams in Budapest[105] now have their own skinhead and fascist fans, with the most popular team, Ferencvaros (FTC)[106] able to marshal several hundred and even more than a thousand on special occasions.[107] In addition, these groups have become increasingly active in organizing demonstrations as well as disrupting others. On March 15, 1992, the commemoration of the 1848 Hungarian revolution was disrupted by skinheads who assaulted the representative of the Roma organization Phralipe and screamed insults at the participants, including Gyorgy Konrad, writer and president of PEN.[108] On September 19, 1992, several hundred skinheads participated in a demonstration of some 10,000 calling for the resignation of the presidents of the state-run TV and radio.[109]

On October 23, 1992 some 800 skinheads, dozens of them wearing Nazi insignia, including the swastika, the Hungarian arrowcross

---

[104] Although there is also an extreme left-wing comprised of, among others, the Leftist Revisionist Party and the May 1 Society, these groups have not thus far engaged in the type of behavior that is the subject of this report.

[105] with the possible exception of MTK, a club traditionally comprised of Jewish players and supporters.

[106] whose supporters have been traditionally associated, stretching back to the pre-Communist era, with nationalist and anti-Semitic ideologies.

[107] A film shot by *Fekete Doboz* (*Black Box*), an independent documentary company, shows dozens of FTC supporters wearing SS uniforms, with hundreds raising their hands in the Hitler salute during a match with a Slovakian team, played on September 12, 1992.

[108] *168 Ora*, March 21, 1992; *Beszelo*, March 21, 1992.

[109] *Magyar Hirlap*, September 21, 1992. A counter-demonstration against racism, organized by the Democratic Charter attracted some 70,000 people. RW report, supra at 11.

emblem and Arpad-stripe decorated armbands,[110] gathered to establish the Independent National Youth Alliance, unifying some half dozen skinhead groups. Subsequently, the skinheads proceeded to the Kossuth square where they disrupted the commemoration of the anniversary of the 1956 uprising and prevented Arpad Goncz, President of the Republic, from delivering his speech.[111] The police units on the site failed to take any action.

On November 30, 1992, skinheads also attempted to attend the dedication of the "turul"-bird monument (a mythical bird) in Tatabanya where the President was to be the key speaker. On this occasion the police took preventive measures and very few skinheads succeeded in evading the police cordons - and there were no disruptions.[112]

These incidents have rekindled the debate about free speech. Many Roma advocates complain that the Constitutional Court's decision of May 1992 to strike down Section 269 (2) of the Penal Code as unconstitutional,[113] though affirming the constitutionality of 269 (1) (which states in effect that incitement to hatred is a criminal offense punishable by up to three years of incarceration), provides too much protection to racist speech. In particular, Roma leaders, human rights advocates and numerous prominent public figures[114] have been pressing for a ban on the display of Nazi symbols. Although Parliament has been debating an amendment to Section 256 for some time,

---

[110] A historical symbol which was appropriated by the Hungarian fascists during the 1930s.

[111] *Nepszabadsag*, October 26, 1992.

[112] *Nepszabadsag*, November 30, 1992.

[113] Section 269 §(2) stated that "any person using in public an expression offending or demeaning the Hungarian nation, any of its minority nations, groups or sects or races, or who commits other similar offenses, will be fined or punished for up to one year of incarceration with corrective labor."

[114] Including some 100 writers. BBC summary of World Broadcast Text of reports EE/1524 B/8, November 6, 1992.

vehement opposition remains as many MPs view the proposed ban as an impermissible chilling of free speech.[115]

But the extreme right elements need no longer rely exclusively on their own press. Fascism and the skinhead phenomenon and violence connected with it has become a major story for "responsible" and sensationalist press alike, both of which provide countless venues for extremists to air their beliefs. *168 Ora*, a weekly radio broadcast and publication, arguably the premier investigative journalist program, has interviewed skinheads, along with Romas, on numerous occasions.[116] Skinhead leaders also appear in television interviews to discuss and analyze the skinhead phenomenon. In one recent interview of this type, "Uncle Potyka" (Istvan Porubszky, leader of the "56 Anti-Fascist & Anti-Bolsheviks Alliance, one of the handful of organized extremist groups (see below)) and his followers appeared on "Thermometer," a regular program on the state-run channel[117] in which several prominent human right advocates and MPs also participated. Some human rights advocates are now voicing concern regarding such media events, arguing that laudatory motivations for engaging in a dialogue notwithstanding, these meetings may have inadvertently helped to legitimate rather than discredit the extremist elements.[118]

Skinheads and self-proclaimed fascists are only one source of ultra-nationalist, racist and xenophobic outpourings, however. Since the 1990 election, a growing number of well-known and powerful figures in Hungarian politics have come to espouse extremist positions. Foremost among them is Istvan Csurka, writer, a former vice-president and chief ideologue of the governing Democratic Forum. Mr Csurka, who believes that Hungary is threatened by an international conspiracy of

---

[115] For example, MP Jozsef Szajer of the opposition Federation of Young Democrats voiced his party's opposition for this reason in the Parliamentary debates of February 8, 1993. See Appendix for Human Rights Watch's policy on the protection of "hate speech."

[116] *e.g.* November 24, 1992 at 8-9.

[117] *Homero*, September 27, 1992, TV2.

[118] See, *e.g.*, "A szavak es a rasszizmus," ("Words and Racism"), *Pro Minoritate*, 1992 X-XI No. 13-14 at 5.

"cosmopolitans" (a euphemism for Jews), bankers, liberals and communists, had the following to say about the Romas in a recent manifesto [119] which has come to be seen by many as reaching the nadir of Hungarian political discourse:

> We must put an end to the sick practice of blaming the skinheads for everything that is wrong, and educate them using police methods while accepting with understanding other sickness, crime, and cultural crimes. It is no longer possible to ignore the fact that there are genetic reasons behind the degeneracy. We must realize that the disadvantaged and severely disadvantaged strata and groups have been living with us for too long, among which the rigor of natural selection does not function because it has no meaning.

Human rights advocates have also been dismayed by what they perceive to have been an inadequate response by the governing coalition. Although the Prime Minister, Mr. Jozsef Antall, distanced himself from the Csurka statement, albeit in a fashion which many critics thought was too tepid,[120] an opposition he has since reiterated,[121] and although some prominent members of his party openly denounced Mr. Csurka's views,[122] support for Mr. Csurka's views is considerable. Among

---

[119] *Magyar Forum*, August 20, 1992.

[120] Stating before Parliament on August 31, 1992 that "in my judgment on numerous questions he [Csurka] applies erroneous interpretations, answering in a politically deleterious and incorrect manner with which neither the government nor I personally can concur."

[121] Most recently in January, 1993 at the MDF's annual national congress and in February, 1993 in meeting with Catherine Lalumiere, Council of Europe Secretary-General. (MTI February 15, 1993). Concurrently, however, the Prime Minister argued that the outcry generated was "exaggerated" and "out of proportion." *Newsweek*, September 28, 1992.

[122] *e.g.*, Jozsef Debreczeni, "Open letter to Istvan Csurka," *Nepszabadsag*, August 27, 1992.

members of parliament, Gyula Zacsek (MDF), author of anti-Semitic tract appearing in *Magyar Forum*[123] and Izabella B. Kiraly (MDF), who has conducted extended discussions with neo-Nazi skinheads in the past, and has defended them in her parliamentary address,[124] are singled out as the most vociferous supporters of Csurka's extremism. Since the delivery of his speech, Mr. Csurka has established the Hungarian Way (Magyar Ut) Foundation, an umbrella group of the extreme right wing of the governing coalition parties whose first congress before some 2,000 included many other MPs, including Istvan Halasz, Zsolt Zetenyi[125] as well as senior party members such Jeno Laszlo and Elemer Farkas.

Public manifestation of anti-Roma, as well as anti-Semitic and xenophobic attitudes are not limited by any means to people viewing themselves as extremists. The perceptions that Romas are criminally inclined, dangerous, filthy, noisy etc. are widely shared and frequently asserted. As one person summed up what may be a widely held view, in a letter to Ottilia Solt:

> I cannot comprehend, even if you're a liberal how could you always and in every circumstance take the Gypsies' side? Have you ever lived in a house with Gypsies? Surely not!! Because that is hell. That everyone harms the poor Gypsy, from the government to the local council, that I've heard often from you, but not the reason why everybody hates them! They cannot live like normal European people, though they had twenty-five to thirty years to become humanized during the communists. Nobody forbade them from working and learning. But they steal and beg instead from childhood on. They teach their children to cheat. There are few exceptions. And don't tell me it's poverty that made them do it because they are not poor. They have money for

---

[123] September 3, 1992, attacking George Soros, a Hungarian-American philanthropist.

[124] *Magyar Hirlap*, September 29, 1992; AFP wire report February 13, 1992 (Lexis).

[125] AFP, February 13, 1993 (Lexis).

everything, from food to taxis . . . in any house where a Gypsy family leaves there can be no peace for a single minute. They'll steal whatever they can, nothing can be left outside not even the doormat.[126]

Violence

Skinheads and other extremist groups

Skinheads first appeared in Hungary during the 1970s and began to organize in the early 1980s in Budapest, Gyor, Szeged, Miskolc and Eger. In 1988, following a series of attacks on journalists and Cuban guestworkers, the police arrested a large number and eventually some fifteen skinheads were jailed until the amnesty of October 23, 1989. Since then, skinheads have been organized into approximately half a dozen mainly regional chapters. The largest of these now include the Black Guard, located in Miskolc with an estimated membership of 100 or so; the Istvan Utasi Fatherland Party's "footmen guards," comprising a few dozen core members; the Independent Smallholder Party's Independent Patriotic Heritage Conservation Section with centers in Eger, Nyiregyhaza and Tatabanya with core membership of some 400-500; the '56 Anti-Fascist and Anti-Communist Alliance with some 100-150 core members; and the OBASZ (Osisegkutati Barantazo Aranykopjasok Szervezet) with perhaps another 100-150 core members.[127] These groups recently sought to create a unified alliance, the Independent National Youth Alliance, founded on October 23, 1992, with some 800 members.[128] In addition, these groups can draw on a substantially larger pool of sympathizers and other extremist organizations.

Skinhead attacks against Romas began in 1990 with the towns of Eger and Miskolc becoming their focus. In September 1990, a Roma man was badly beaten and in May 1991, some 150 skinheads attacked Romas in a pogrom-like assault in Eger, followed by other large-scale attacks

---

[126] *Beszelo*, November 30, 1991 letter to the editor.

[127] *Uj Hirnok*, May 18, 1992; *168 Ora*, November 24, 1992; *Nepszabadsag*, November 23, 1992; *White Book*, supra; Zoltan Gal interview supra.

[128] *Nepszabadsag*, September 26, 1992.

involving dozens of skinheads in October 1991 and smaller scale attacks (fewer than ten) in August 1992.[129] During 1992 the number of assaults appears to have increased, although reliable estimates are not available.

The police investigated only some six attacks against Romas and foreign students during 1991[130] and initiated a total of eleven criminal proceedings against 111 defendants between January 1991 and January 1993, including the forty-eight defendants in the "skinhead trial" discussed above.[131] During the first half of 1992, the police reported some sixteen attacks on foreigners and five on Romas,[132] in contrast with the Martin Luther King Association's documentation of forty-eight. For the year overall, the police registered some thirty-seven skinhead attacks[133] compared with the 100 or so cases that were registered by the Martin Luther King Association.[134] However, the number of skinhead attacks on Romas appear to be higher than the MLK estimate, given that many Romas do not report an attack to the police. The extent of non-reporting is difficult to estimate, though Roma advocates suggest that no more than one in five cases is reported. Journalists tracking skinhead activities also suggest that the number of incidents is higher than indicated either by the police or the MLK figures; some sources suggest that, on average, there are a couple of attacks in Budapest per week, coupled with less frequent but recurring assaults in Miskolc, Eger, Gyor, Tatabanya, Nyiregyhaza - which would yield approximately 200 attacks for 1992.[135]

---

[129] *White Book*; *Beszelo*, September 26, 1992.

[130] Janos Bodracska, Chief of Budapest Police, *Nepszabadsag*, March 6, 1992.

[131] MTI News service January 25, 1993.

[132] Gyorgy Gabriel, reported in the *White Book*.

[133] *Nepszabadsag*, January 18, 1993.

[134] The reliability of police statistics has been criticized, among others, by the police themselves as well as the Budapest Prosecutor's office. *Beszelo*, November 14, 1992.

[135] Helsinki Watch interview with Zoltan Gal. Also *168 Ora*, August 25, 1992 at 16, claiming that human rights advocates know of ten times as many assaults as the police registers.

In Budapest, the Kobanya-Kispest subway station was the site of a January 1992 skinhead attack against two Nigerians in which one of the assailants was fatally wounded. In response, skinheads initiated about two dozen attacks against foreign students and Romas over the next few weeks.[136] The district had already become notorious for skinhead attacks: Cuban guestworkers were beaten there in 1988, an attack resulting in prison terms for several skinheads, and some sixty skinheads attacked Nigerian students and Romas in January 1991, causing serious injury to three Nigerians and about a dozen Romas.[137] Other large-scale anti-Roma assaults took place in May 1992 and January 1993, following which eight skinheads were arrested.[138]

But large-scale brawls between skinheads and Romas appear to be the exception rather than the rule. More common are assaults on individuals, often taking place in the evening at deserted bus, streetcar or subway stations or carriages. Ilona V., a woman who was beaten by a skinhead, described her ordeal to Helsinki Watch:

> It was January 8 [1993] around 11 p.m. at the Ors vezer square where I caught the bus when some six or eight skinheads got on . . . I think they were drunk and they began to look for someone to annoy. Initially one of them picked on a rocker with long hair but the others stopped him, saying that Magyars must not be beaten, only Gypsies, Negroes or traitors. Then the old man sitting next to me got off and one of the skins, I think he was no more than sixteen or seventeen sat down, looked at me and hit me with his fist so my head smashed against the plate, saying that I am a filthy Gypsy. I turned around to ask for help but the young guy sitting behind me just shrugged his shoulders. Someone else got on, but did nothing either. The other skinheads were not interested either. I begged him to stop so he put his hand around my throat and hit my head against the glass

---

[136] MLK figure.

[137] See above; also *Beszelo*, July 11, 1992.

[138] MTI, January 23, 1993.

repeatedly . . . But then I began to cry that I am not a Gypsy and one of the skins took a look and said "look here, she is a Magyar, not a Gypsy" and told the guy to stop hitting me . . . the guy then began to cry and apologize to me profusely saying that he never wanted to hurt a Magyar and reprimanded me for not telling him sooner that I wasn't a Gypsy.

Ilona, who still had bruises on her neck, did not report the incident to the police, saying that it never occurred to her that the police could do anything. "Besides," she added, "if I go to the police then everyone else would know that they thought I was a Gypsy and that would be humiliating to my parents."

Similar skinhead attacks have taken place in Miskolc. As one taxi-driver told Helsinki Watch:

Years ago it was said that it wasn't safe for a non-Gypsy to walk through the city center [which was adjacent to a large Roma slum] after dark because they would be harassed by the Gypsies. Now it's the other way around, and Gypsies can't walk at night without being hassled.

Salgotarjan, a city near Eger, has also seen an increase in skinhead attacks. It was here that on November 6, 1992, a 15-year-old military cadet and his 16-year-old accomplice used a baseball bat to beat to death Zoltan Danyi, a 32-year-old Roma man. Both youths were arrested. The younger one committed suicide some three weeks later while in detention awaiting trial. Criminal proceedings are pending against the second youth.[139]

The impact of these attacks has reached beyond the immediate victims as many Romas now increasingly live in fear. The terrorization of Romas, many of their leaders warn, may trigger further violence if Romas begin to fight back. As Aladar Horvath, President of the Roma Parliament, explained to Helsinki Watch:

---

[139] *Nepszabadsag*, November 10, 1992; *Beszelo*, November 14 and December 5, 1992; *168 Ora*, November 24, 1992.

Parts of the city, and parts of the country, too, are now gripped by terror. What happened in places like Nyirtabor [see above] could happen elsewhere, too, as ghettoes are becoming a powder keg of fear ready to explode if the skinhead attacks are not dealt with more forcefully by the police.

Other Roma leaders, though, maintain that Romas are far from cowering in fear and that predictions of Roma vigilante backlash are baseless. As Gyula Naday, leader of MCDSZ, a rival of the Horvath-led Roma Parliament, argued to Helsinki Watch:

The situation is bad but not as critical as some Gypsy leaders would have you believe . . . I don't believe that most of our people live in fear, and anyhow it's irresponsible to feed or create a mass hysteria.

Other attacks and communal strife

While skinhead attacks represent the bulk of anti-Roma violence, other types of attacks have been recently surfacing which rarely espouse the skinhead's overt racism but whose motives frequently have racist underpinnings. The most tragic such case was the 1992 shooting of a Roma woman and man by a forest guard who caught four Romas stealing pears fallen from the trees.[140] Although the exact circumstances remain disputed, and criminal proceeding are pending, several witnesses claimed that the guard had threatened in the past to "do away with Gypsy thieves." Eyewitnesses stated that it was an execution-style killing with the woman shot in the stomach at close range, while the second victim was killed while trying to flee the scene. The guard maintains that both deaths were accidental shootings.[141]

The double killing occurred less than a week after the outbreak of communal strife in Ketegyhaza, a village near the Romanian border inhabited by Hungarian Romas, non-Romas (accounting for some 15 percent of the population) as well as Romanians. On September 7, 1992,

---

[140] *Magyar Hirlap*, September 14, 1992.

[141] *Nepszabadsag*, January 5, 1993.

Peter Csurar, Jr., a Roma inhabitant of the village, had an altercation with Mihaly Gulyas, a non-Roma resident. In the ensuing fight, which was joined by a number of supporters on both sides, Mr. Gulyas suffered a cut to his head. The brawl was ended when the police were called, but at dawn the following day six men, including Mihaly Gulyas and his brother, used a truck to ram the house of Peter Csurar, who fled his home. The Csurars were then hounded and one of them was badly beaten. The police re-entered the village, but later that night three Molotov cocktails were thrown at three Csurar homes, two of which were destroyed. The police then arrested five non-Romas[142] and, later the next day, four of the Csurars. The village's non-Roma population began to demonstrate, calling for the release of the five arrested people and called on the mayor and the police to remove all three Csurar families for good. The four arrested Csurars were later released, but were told by the police to stay with relatives in another village. A few days later an order was issued to demolish all three houses as a safety risk and the Csurar families were forced to leave the village. Subsequently, nearly two dozen villagers were charged with various offenses ranging from disturbing the peace to causing loss of property, but no one was charged with arson.[143]

The arson and subsequent eviction of the Csurar family from the village has led to bitter accusations, denials, as well as much soul-searching.[144] For two days, as the village remained on the precipice with locals demonstrating for the ouster of the Csurars, the police came under fire from all sides for their failure to prevent the violence. Non-Romas threatened to take matters into their own hands if the law would not protect them from the "trouble-makers" while the Roma inhabitants complained that they were being terrorized by the local non-Roma

---

[142] *Beszelo*, December 19, 1992; other accounts give the number of initial arrests as six, e.g., *Magyar Hirlap*, September 10, 1992 and September 11, 1992 and *Magyar Narancs*, September 17, 1992.

[143] *Beszelo*, December 19, 1992.

[144] The events at Ketegyhaza were extensively reported. *See, e.g., Beszelo*, September 19 and 26 and December 19, 1992; *Magyar Hirlap*, September 10, 11, 12 and 15, October 5 and December 2 and 12, 1992; *Nepszabdsag*, September 9, 10, 12, 14, 15, 17, 19 and 28 and October 5, 9 and 15, 1992; *Magyar Nemzet*, September 10, 1992; *Magyar Narancs*, September 17, 1992.

vigilantes.[145] Police officials deflected these criticisms, arguing that they lacked the manpower required to prevent eruption of local conflicts. The Minister of the Interior, Peter Boross, used Ketegyhaza as an example to illustrate the need for preventive police raids. He also chided the media for inaccurate reporting of the strife, and politicians for rushing to the scene, suggesting that their presence exacerbated the conflict.[146] This criticism, coupled with suggestions by the Minister that the attacks were not manifestly racist in nature, or - as suggested by other MPs - that the arson was an unlawful but essentially defensive measure,[147] incensed many Roma leaders and human rights advocates who countered that the minister's own recital of facts was erroneous and that the arson attack could not be characterized as other than racially motivated.[148]

To what extent Ketegyhaza should be regarded as an aberration or as an early warning of ethnic strife ready to explode remains hotly debated. The pessimistic assessment of many Roma leaders is challenged by the Minister of the Interior's conclusion that Ketegyhaza does not represent a trend at all.[149] However, the majority view, including that of many government officials, appears to be less sanguine. As Janos Bathory, Deputy Chief of the Office of National and Ethnic Minorities, discussing Tura and Ketegyhaza, explained to Helsinki Watch:

> That a guard shoots a Gypsy or two, this is tragic, but I don't view that as ethnic conflict because in one year there are some twenty or thirty such episodes in Hungary . . . that the victims happened to be Gypsies is not the issue . . . but Ketegyhaza is more interesting . .

---

[145] *Magyar Hirlap*, October 5, 1992.

[146] Minutes of Parliament, September 14, 1992, at 19077-78; *Magyar Hirlap*, September 15, 1992.

[147] Zoltan Varga (MDF), Minutes of Parliament, September 14, 1992 at 19087.

[148] On the factual errors in the Minister's recital see *Beszelo*, December 19, 1992.

[149] "I would like to point out that Ketegyhaza and Tura is not a general phenomenon; no colorable claim can be made that this is an ethnic war."

. there were definitely ethnic motives in the episode. . .
and such Gypsy-Magyar conflict is growing, though there
are very great regional differences. There are regions
where such conflicts are everyday occurrences, especially
in the north of Hungary such as Borsod . . . and there
are specific places such as, for example, Ozd, where the
threat of another Ketegyhaza looms large.[150]

Gabor Demszky, the mayor of Budapest, also told Helsinki Watch
that Ketegyhaza was unlikely to be the last such outbreak of ethnic strife:

Unfortunately, my impression in the past year and a half
is that there is definitely a growing tendency at work
rather than an isolated episode . . . and society is not
prepared to tackle this issue. On the contrary, people are
exhausted, apathetic, they have become so focused on
their own survival . . . that they just don't want to deal
with this issue.[151]

But even among those who agree that ethnic strife is unlikely to
abate, the analyses of the causes differ. Some believe that there are
Romas in many villages who act as the Csurar family's younger members
allegedly behaved - that is, as bullies harassing the local population. As
Janos Bathory stated to Helsinki Watch:

There are places in northern Hungary where the
majority of villagers are Gypsies and where the majority
of non-Gypsies are elderly people . . . Here, and we don't
talk of this issue much in public, the Gypsies literally
terrorize the elderly and practically there is nothing
anyone is willing to do about it. There are instances
when the Gypsies go into a Magyar household and drag

---

[150] Helsinki Watch interview, January 14, 1993.

[151] Helsinki Watch interview, January 15, 1993.

out the chickens or a pig, in front of everyone, and simply take it.[152]

Others disagree, arguing that to single out a number of Roma families in strife-ridden villages as the major cause of tensions is scapegoating. The main problems, such critics maintain, are the worsening economic conditions coupled with growing legitimization of the use of force and the increasing respectability of overt racism. As Janos Ladanyi summed up to Helsinki Watch:

> The reason why Gypsy homes are burnt down is not because no other way can be found to deal with local trouble-makers, but because villagers accurately gauge the mood of the country today, which is one of loathing for foreigners, - and Gypsies, too, are deemed foreigners by most Magyars - and because these villagers see that many Magyars sympathize with the skinheads they now realize that beating and evicting Gypsies can be done with impunity.

---

[152] Helsinki Watch interview, January 14, 1993.

INTERNATIONAL LAW

International law protects the right of individuals to belong to an ethnic or national minority, and to express, preserve, and develop their cultural traditions:

> To belong to a national minority is a matter of a person's individual choice and no disadvantage may arise from the exercise of such choice. Persons belonging to national minorities have the right freely to express, preserve and develop their ethnic, cultural, linguistic or religious identity and to maintain and develop their culture in all its aspects, free of any attempts at assimilation against their will. (Document of the Copenhagen Meeting of the Conference on the Human Dimension of the CSCE (1990), Paragraph 32.)

> The participating States. . . reaffirm that respect for the rights of persons belonging to national minorities as part of universally recognized human rights is an essential factor for peace, justice, stability and democracy in the participating States. (Document of the Copenhagen Meeting of the Conference on the Human Dimension of the CSCE (1990), Paragraph 30.)

International law prohibits states from discriminating on the basis of ethnic or national identity, and requires states to take positive measures to prevent discrimination on these grounds:

> All are equal before the law and are entitled without any discrimination to equal protection of the law. (Universal Declaration of Human Rights (1948), Article 7.)

> All persons are equal before the law and are entitled without any discrimination to the equal protection of the law. In this respect, the law shall prohibit any discrimination and guarantee to all persons equal and effective protection against discrimination on any ground such as race, color, sex, language, religion,

57

political or other opinion, national or social origin, property, birth or other status. (International Covenant on Civil and Political Rights (1966), Article 26, signed by Hungary on March 25, 1969 and ratified on January 17, 1974.)

The participating States will adopt, where necessary, special measures for the purpose of ensuring to persons belonging to national minorities full equality with the other citizens in the exercise and enjoyment of human rights and fundamental freedoms. (Document of the Copenhagen Meeting of the Conference on the Human Dimension of the CSCE (1990), Paragraph 31.)

States have an obligation to protect all citizens from violence, including a specific obligation to protect minorities from violence due to racial or ethnic identity:

States Parties undertake to prohibit and to eliminate racial discrimination in all its forms and to guarantee the right of everyone without distinction as to race, color, or national origin, to equality before the law, notably in the enjoyment of . . .

b. The right to security of person and protection by the State against violence or bodily harm, whether inflicted by Government officials or by any individual, group, or institution. . . (United Nations International Convention on the Elimination of All Forms of Racial Discrimination (1966), Article 5, signed by Hungary on September 15, 1966 and ratified on May 4, 1967.)

The participating States . . . commit themselves to take appropriate and proportionate measures to protect persons or groups who may be subject to threats or acts of discrimination, hostility or violence as a result of their racial, ethnic, cultural, linguistic or religious identity, and to protect their property . . . (Document of the Copenhagen Meeting of the Conference on the Human Dimension of the CSCE (1990), Paragraph 40.2.)

In 1990 in Copenhagen, the CSCE countries (i.e., the countries that signed the Helsinki Final Act and follow-up documents, among them Hungary) specifically recognized the problems of Gypsies, and pledged to take measures to remedy them:

> The participating States clearly and unequivocally condemn totalitarianism, racial and ethnic hatred, anti-semitism, xenophobia and discrimination against anyone as well as persecution on religious and ideological grounds. In this context, they also recognize the particular problems of Roma (Gypsies). They declare their firm intention to intensify the efforts to combat these phenomena in all their forms . . . (Document of the Copenhagen Meeting of the Conference on the Human Dimension of the CSCE (1990), Paragraph 40.)

All citizens have the right to take part in public affairs:

> Every citizen shall have the right and the opportunity [without distinction of any kind, such as race, colour, sex, language, religion, political or other opinion, national or social origin, property, birth or other status] . . . and without unreasonable restrictions: (a) To take part in the conduct of public affairs, directly or through freely chosen representatives . . . (International Covenant on Civil and Political Rights (1966), Article 25.)

International law allows parents the right to choose the kind of education that shall be given to their children:

> Everyone has the right to education . . . Elementary education shall be compulsory. Technical and professional education shall be made generally available and higher education shall be equally accessible to all on the basis of merit . . . Parents have a prior right to choose the kind of education that shall be given to their children. (Universal Declaration of Human Rights (1948), Article 26.)

International law requires states to ensure that minorities have adequate opportunities for instruction in their mother tongue:

> The participating States will protect the ethnic, cultural, linguistic and religious identity of national minorities on their territory and create conditions for the promotion of that identity. (Document of the Copenhagen Meeting of the Conference on the Human Dimension of the CSCE (1990), Paragraph 33.)

> The participating States will endeavour to ensure that persons belonging to national minorities, notwithstanding the need to learn the official language or languages of the State concerned, have adequate opportunities for instruction of their mother tongue or in their mother tongue, as well as, wherever possible and necessary, for its use before public authorities, in conformity with applicable national legislation. (Document of the Copenhagen Meeting of the Conference on the Human Dimension of the CSCE (1990), Paragraph 34.)

International law requires states to take account of the history and culture of national minorities when preparing curricula, and to take other measures to promote racial and ethnic tolerance through education:

> In the context of the teaching of history and culture in educational establishments, [the participating States] will . . . take account of the history and culture of national minorities. (Document of the Copenhagen Meeting of the Conference on the Human Dimension of the CSCE (1990), Paragraph 34.)

> The participating States [will] . . . endeavour to ensure that the objectives of education include special attention to the problem of racial prejudice and hatred and to the development of respect for different civilizations and cultures . . . (Document of the Copenhagen Meeting of the Conference on the Human Dimension of the CSCE (1990), Paragraph 40.4.)

Education shall be directed to the full development of the human personality and to the strengthening of respect for human rights and fundamental freedoms. It shall promote understanding, tolerance and friendship among all nations, racial or religious groups, and shall further the activities of the United Nations for the maintenance of peace. (Universal Declaration of Human Rights (1948), Article 26.)

International law requires states to take additional measures to promote mutual understanding and tolerance:

Every participating State will promote a climate of mutual respect, understanding, co-operation and solidarity among all persons living on its territory, without distinction as to ethnic or national origin or religion, and will encourage the solution of problems through dialogue based on the principles of the rule of law. (Document of the Copenhagen Meeting of the Conference on the Human Dimension of the CSCE (1990), Paragraph 36.)

The participating States [will] . . . take effective measures, in conformity with their constitutional systems, at the national, regional and local levels to promote understanding and tolerance, particularly in the fields of education, culture and information . . . (Document of the Copenhagen Meeting of the Conference on the Human Dimension of the CSCE (1990), Paragraph 40.3.)

International law allows states to take special measures (i.e., "affirmative action"), for a limited period of time, to ensure members of all ethnic groups the equal enjoyment and exercise of human rights and fundamental freedoms:

Special measures taken for the sole purpose of securing adequate advancement of certain racial or ethnic groups or individuals requiring such protection as may be necessary in order to ensure such groups or individuals equal enjoyment or exercise of human rights and fundamental freedoms shall not be deemed racial discrimination, provided, however, that such measures do not, as a consequence, lead to the maintenance of separate rights for different racial groups and that they shall not be continued after the objectives for which they were taken have been achieved. (International Convention on the Elimination of All Forms of Racial Discrimination (1966), Article 1.)

International law obliges states to undertake to eliminate racial discrimination:

I.   States Parties condemn racial discrimination and undertake to pursue by all appropriate means and without delay a policy of eliminating racial discrimination in all its forms and promoting understanding among all races, and, to this end:

a) Each State Party undertakes to engage in no act or practice of racial discrimination against persons, groups of persons, or institutions and to ensure that all public authorities and public institutions, national and local, shall act in conformity with this obligation;

b) Each State Party undertakes not to sponsor, defend or support racial discrimination by any persons or organizations;

c)   Each State Party shall take effective measures to review governmental, national, and local policies, and to amend, rescind, or nullify any laws and regulations which have the effect of creating or perpetuating racial discrimination wherever it exists;

d) Each State Party shall prohibit and bring to an end, by all appropriate means, including legislation as required by circumstances, racial discrimination by any persons, group or organization;

e) Each State Party undertakes to encourage, where appropriate, integrationist multi-racial organizations and movements and other means of eliminating barriers between races, and to discourage anything which tends to strengthen racial division. (International Convention on the Elimination of All Forms of Racial Discrimination (1966), Article 2)

International law requires States to guarantee victims of racial discrimination an effective remedy:

States Parties shall assure to everyone within their jurisdiction effective protection and remedies, through the competent national tribunals and other State institutions, against any acts of racial discrimination which violate his human rights and fundamental freedoms contrary to this Convention, as well as the right to seek from such tribunals just and adequate reparation or satisfaction for any damage suffered as a result of such discrimination. (International Convention on the Elimination of All Forms of Racial Discrimination (1966), Article 6.)

The conduct of police officers is prescribed by international standards:

Law enforcement officials shall at all times fulfill the duty imposed upon them by law, by serving the community and by protecting all persons against

illegal acts, consistent with the high degree of responsibility required by their profession.[153]

In the performance of their duty, law enforcement officials shall respect and protect human dignity and

---

[153] United Nations Code of Conduct for Law Enforcement Officials, Article 1.

maintain and uphold the human rights of all persons.[154]

The government of Hungary has a responsibility to guarantee that police officers have the proper training and equipment to fulfill their obligations, and that those obligations are carried out promptly, fairly and without discrimination. Specifically, the government has an obligation to make clear to police officers which means may be used to prevent the commission of a crime, and the circumstances under which particular means are appropriate.

Governments should make human rights and civil rights training a part of any police training program:

> In the training of law enforcement officials, Governments and law enforcement agencies shall give special attention to issues of police ethics and human rights, especially in the investigative process, to alternatives to the use of force and firearms, including the peaceful settlement of conflicts, the understanding of crowd behavior, and the methods of persuasion, negotiation and mediation, as well as to technical means, with a view to limiting the use of force and firearms. Law enforcement agencies should review their training programs and operational procedures in the light of particular incidents.[155]

In cases where allegations are made of police misconduct, it is the duty of the responsible authorities to conduct an investigation and carry out the appropriate disciplinary measures.

> Every law enforcement agency . . . should be held to the duty of disciplining itself . . . and the actions of law

---

[154] *Ibid.*, Article 2.

[155] *Ibid.*, Article 20.

enforcement officials should be responsive to public scrutiny.[156]

---

[156] Preamble to the United Nations Code of Conduct for Law Enforcement Officials.

CONCLUSIONS

The situation of Hungary's Romas has changed dramatically since the fall of the communist regime. Much of this change has been positive: after four decades of repression, aspirations for developing and manifesting ethnic and cultural identity are now blossoming, as evidenced by the proliferation of Roma cultural, social and political organizations and publications, as well as the rebirth of teaching of the Romany language. The bygone era's aggressive assimilationism, its paternalist absolutism and proselytization of the inferiority of the "Gypsy" way of life and values, an ideology inculcated in tens of thousands who became convinced of their own worthlessness, has now been abandoned. Overtly racist and anti-Roma measures, notably the "Gypsy-criminality police units," have been abandoned. A new legal order is in the process of being put in place, based upon the recognition of and respect for Roma rights. The Constitution recognizes equality of Romas, their rights - as one of Hungary's national and ethnic minorities - to express, preserve and develop their cultural traditions and mandates the enactment of affirmative measures to achieve equality for Romas.

But realization of that goal has proved elusive and only part of this failure can be attributed to the failings of the past regimes. The economic restructuring necessitated by jettisoning of the command economy created large-scale unemployment among all Hungarians. But for Romas, generally constituting the worst paid and least trained workers, the economic transition has become an immediate crisis, further aggravated by discrimination in the labor market which disproportionately singles out Roma workers for dismissals. As a consequence, three quarters of adult Roma men are unemployed and a new generation is reared with the knowledge that their prospects for finding a decent job are grim. In addition, the inescapable reliance on unemployment benefits and a desperate poverty which occasionally forces some Romas to resort to petty crime exacerbates other Hungarians' deep-seated prejudices against the Romas, long portrayed as "lazy" and "criminal."

The promise of complete legal equality likewise remains unfulfilled. Although after years of delay the Minority Bill is on the verge of becoming a reality, the scope of rights conferred and the manner in which they are to be effected is far from clarified. Meanwhile, Romas are faced with tremendous obstacles in exercising their rights in virtually

66

every aspect of life. In applying for public housing or having their grievances adjudicated, Romas are systematically discriminated against by local councils. Discrimination in the labor market is rampant, though covert, and Romas have limited means to seek redress and little success in obtaining it. Exclusion from public places, such as bars, restaurants and discoes is frequent, and propagators of such discriminatory practices are not prosecuted. Police harrassment of Romas exists as well on a systematic basis. Romas are disproportionate victims of unlawful arrests, detentions - often in conditions which violate international law - and occasional beatings. There is also substantial evidence that the police engaged in abusive conduct during a number of commando-style raids on Roma settlements in 1991 and 1992, in violation of Hungary's obligations under international law.

Romas are also subjected to virulent outbreaks of racism. Though most of these outbreaks are confined to the proliferation of anti-Roma (as well as anti-Semitic, anti-Arab and anti-foreigner) articles, cartoons and graffiti, physical violence aimed at Romas is on the rise. The primary source of this violence is Hungary's militant and fervently nationalistic youth, predominantly though not exclusively centered around a few thousand skinheads. Skinhead attacks on Romas have been increasing and much of the blame for the intensification of these attacks rests squarely with the government and the police, neither of which has responded with the required firmness. Government officials, though for the most part condemning such attacks, have displayed no sense of urgency in combatting the violence and, in fact, a small number of influential members of the coalition government have expressed muted - and in some cases overt - support for the skinheads. Likewise, until recently the police showed little zeal in investigating or prosecuting skinheads, although there are some signs that this trend may now be reversing.

RECOMMENDATIONS

Helsinki Watch urges the Hungarian government to:

Abide by its obligations under international law to respect and promote human rights and specifically to:

- Guarantee the security of all persons from violence or bodily harm, whether inflicted by Government officials or by any individual or group.

- Conduct a criminal investigation into each incidence of violence against the Roma community and prosecute to the fullest extent of the law those cases where there is evidence of guilt.

- Investigate allegations that, in certain cases, the Hungarian authorities failed to intervene to protect Romas from attack or failed to adequately investigate violence against Romas, and take all appropriate measures up to and including criminal prosecution.

- Prohibit all forms of discrimination against Romas, including harassment and intimidation by government officials. Provide all citizens with effective administrative and judicial remedies against discrimination.

- Assure Romas the right to equal participation in local administration and local government.

- Guarantee Romas equal rights, in policy and practice, to education.

- Guarantee Romas, in policy and practice, equal access to housing.

- Guarantee Romas equal access to public services and accomodations, including public and private restaurants, discos and bars.

- Guarantee Romas equality in the workplace, and conduct a full investigation into allegations of discriminatory hiring practices.

- Ensure that the Roma minority has adequate opportunities to learn the Romani language. Optional Romani language classes should be offered in elementary and secondary schools.

• Include teaching about the history and culture of Romas in secondary and elementary schools.

• Direct the state-controlled television and radio to provide objective and balanced reporting when airing stories about Roma.

Police and Civil Guards

The government of Hungary has a responsibility to ensure that law enforcement officials fulfill their obligations promptly, fairly and without discrimination. Helsinki Watch urges the Hungarian government to:

• Wherever possible, establish permanent police precincts in place of the civil guards.

• Where civil guards are formed, establish procedures to ensure that members of the civil guards are properly trained and are familiar with their legal duties.

• Ensure that civil guards do not have access to weapons and that their activities are co-ordinated with and supervised by the local police force.

• Make a special effort to recruit Romas and give them an equal opportunity for participation in law enforcement.

• Provide special sensitivity training for all law enforcement officials in human rights and civil rights.

• All allegations of police and/or civil guards' misconduct should be systematically investigated. The number of complaints, the status and results of investigations, as well as any disciplinary actions taken, should be made available to the public.

Ombudsman for human rights

As this report was going to press, the Hungarian parliament passed legislation creating the position of National and Ethnic Minority Ombudsman. Helsinki Watch urges the ombudsman to:

- Collect, collate and investigate human rights and civil rights abuses in every walk of life.

- Make the documentation gathered widely accessible, not only to members of Parliament, but also to the public.

- Where appropriate make such documentation available to the public prosecutor to initiate legal proceedings against parties violating Romas' human and civil rights.

- Establish regional and local ombudsmen to report to regional or local councils, in addition to the central ombudsman.

APPENDIX
HUMAN RIGHTS WATCH POLICY STATEMENT ON
THE PROTECTION OF "HATE SPEECH"

Human Rights Watch condemns all forms of discrimination on such arbitrary grounds as nationality, race, gender or religion. In many countries, anti-discrimination efforts take the form of laws penalizing the communication of group hatred on these or other grounds.

Such laws are often justified on the grounds that they curb racial and ethnic violence. But there is little evidence that they achieve their stated purpose, and they have often been subject to abuse. Many governments and other actors that encourage or exploit group tensions use "hate speech" laws as a pretext to advance a separate political agenda or to enhance their own political power. In a number of countries, the chief targets of "hate speech" laws have been minority rights activists fighting discrimination by the same majority that administers the laws -- or, as in the case of South Africa, by the dominant minority.

Human Rights Watch believes that such laws raise serious freedom of expression issues. We are mindful of the fact that international human rights law provides different and conflicting standards in this area, and base our policy on a strong commitment to freedom of expression as a core principle of human rights. We believe that freedom of speech and equal protection of the laws are not incompatible, but are, rather, mutually reinforcing rights.

We therefore view as suspect any action by governments to criminalize any expression short of incitement to illegal action (as defined below) and consider any law or prosecution that is not based on a strict interpretation of incitement to be presumptively a violation of the right of free expression.

In evaluating "hate speech" laws and prosecutions to ensure that they do not infringe on rights of freedom of expression, Human Rights Watch will take the following factors into account:

(1) Expression should never be punished for its subject matter or content alone, no matter how offensive it may be to others.

(2) Any restriction on the content of expression must be based on direct and immediate incitement of acts of violence,

71

discrimination or hostility against an individual or clearly defined group of persons in circumstances in which such violence, discrimination or hostility is imminent and alternative measures to prevent such conduct are not reasonably available. For this purpose, "violence" refers to physical attack; "discrimination" refers to the actual deprivation of a benefit to which similarly situated people are entitled or the imposition of a penalty or sanction not imposed on other similarly situated people; and "hostility" refers to criminal harassment and criminal intimidation.

(3) Reasonable limitations on the time, place and manner of expression shall not be enforced so as to prevent the effective communication of any information or point of view. The means chosen to implement such limitations should be the least restrictive available to accomplish a legitimate end unrelated to the content of the expression.

(4) Abusive conduct may not be insulated from punishment simply because it may be accompanied by expression, nor may it be singled out for punishment or punished more heavily because of the expression.

In some countries, government agencies and officials engage in verbal attacks on racial and ethnic minorities. We strongly condemn such behavior by government. To the extent that expression is controlled by the government as a means of implementing discriminatory official policy, we do not view it as protected by the free speech principles set forth above.